Bridging Cultures

between Home and School

A GUIDE FOR TEACHERS

Bridging Cultures
Cultures
between Home and School

A GUIDE FOR TEACHERS

with a special focus on immigrant Latino families

Elise Trumbull, Ed.D.
Carrie Rothstein-Fisch, Ph.D.
Patricia M. Greenfield, Ph.D.
Blanca Quiroz, M.A.

with

Marie Altchech, M.A.
Catherine Daley, M.F.A.
Kathryn Eyler
Elvia Hernandez
Giancarlo Mercado
Amada Irma Pérez, M.A.
Pearl Saitzyk

WestEd   This book is a product of the *Bridging Cultures Project*, a collaboration among WestEd, University of California, Los Angeles, California State University, Northridge, and seven teachers from six Los Angeles area schools. Preparation was supported by federal funds from the U.S. Department of Education, Office of Educational Research and Improvement, contract number RJ96006901. Its contents do not necessarily reflect the views or policies of the Department of Education, nor does mention of trade numbers, commercial products, or organizations imply endorsement by the United States Government.

LAWRENCE ERLBAUM ASSOCIATES, PUBLISHERS
2001   Mahwah, New Jersey   London

Lawrence Erlbaum Associates, Inc., Publishers
10 Industrial Avenue
Mahwah, NJ 07430

Cover design by Kathryn Houghtaling Lacey

Library of Congress Cataloging-in-Publication Data

Bridging cultures between home and school : a guide for teachers : with special focus on
    immigrant Latino families / Elise Trumbull ... [et al.].
    p. cm.
      Includes bibliographical references (p.) and index.
    ISBN 0-8058-3519-9 (pbk. : alk. paper)
    Home and school—United States. 2. Parent-teacher relationships—United States. 3. Multicul-
    tural education—United States. 4. Children of immigrants—Education—United States. 5.
    Latinos—Education—United States. I. Trumbull, Elise.
    LC1099.3 .B74   2001
    370.117′0973—dc21   00-051404
                                                                               CIP

Books published by Lawrence Erlbaum Associates are printed
on acid-free paper, and their bindings are chosen for strength
and durability.

Printed in the United States of America
10 9 8 7 6 5

Author Affiliation

Elise Trumbull, Ed.D.
Culture and Language in Education Program
WestEd
San Francisco, California

Carrie Rothstein-Fisch, Ph.D.
Department of Educational Psychology and Counseling
College of Education
California State University, Northridge, California

Patricia M. Greenfield, Ph.D.
Department of Psychology
University of California, Los Angeles, California

Blanca Quiroz, M.A.
Department of Psychology and Latin American Studies Program
University of California, Los Angeles, California
(now a doctoral candidate, Department of Psychology and Human Development, Harvard University, Cambridge, Massachusetts)

Los Angeles Unified School District, Los Angeles, California
Marie Altchech, M.A., Stoner Ave. Elementary School
Catherine Daley, M.F.A., Magnolia Elementary School
Kathryn Eyler, Hoover Ave. Elementary School
Giancarlo Mercado, Westminster Ave. Elementary School
Pearl Saitzyk, Westminster Ave. Elementary School

Los Nietos School District, Whittier, California
Elvia Hernandez, Ada S. Nelson Elementary School

Ocean View School District, Oxnard, California
Amada Irma Pérez, M.A., Mar Vista Elementary School

We dedicate this book to the immigrant students and their families, who deal so valiantly with uprooting and transplantation.

Contents

Preface

RESPONDING TO THE INCREASE
IN CLASSROOM DIVERSITY

It is not news to most people that classrooms around the United States are becoming more and more culturally and linguistically diverse. Some teachers have relatively homogeneous classrooms but with students whose primary language and/or cultural background are much different from their own. Others find themselves in classrooms with students from numerous cultural backgrounds — at various stages of proficiency with English and at multiple academic levels. Still other teachers, working in schools just beginning to become diverse, realize that teaching their new students successfully is going to mean learning about new cultures.

Parallel to these demographic changes and consequent concerns is a renewed recognition that our society has always been diverse. American Indian and African-American students have been part of this diversity, although for many generations they were segregated from the dominant group. More recently, Alaska Native and Pacific Island students have added to the diversity. People from Asian countries (beginning largely with the Chinese and then the Japanese) began arriving in this country 150 years ago, although they were denied citizenship for almost 100 years; and in recent decades, the whole concept of "Asian-American" has been broadened to include immigrants from Korea, Vietnam, Cambodia, Laos, and Malaysia, as well as India and other countries. There are also sizeable communities of Arab-Americans in certain parts of the country, the Midwest, for example. The list could go on, if we were to do justice to the reality of diversity in the United States.

European-Americans themselves are a more diverse group than is normally recognized, including peoples whose ethnic and religious identities are distinct. In addition to ethnic and cultural differences, class differences influence not only life opportunities (e.g., access to schooling, housing, jobs) but also values surrounding child-rearing and schooling. So, along with efforts to understand the cultures of the newer immigrants, we have the opportunity to investigate how schooling might serve the needs of a population that is much more diverse than is usually acknowledged.

Teachers throughout the country are begging for professional development opportunities to help them meet the challenges of teaching this diverse population. Yet the kind of support teachers need to understand their new students and their students' communities is not always available. It requires more than sensitivity training or courses on the histories of ethnic groups. Teachers need frameworks that help explain the deep value orientations underlying the beliefs and behaviors of different cultures. They need examples that can demonstrate not just particular cultural practices but the *role* of cultural values in learning, schooling, and child-rearing. The *Bridging Cultures* framework fills this gap.

It is generally agreed that parent involvement in children's schooling is the linchpin of student success. However, engaging parents from so-called "minority" communities requires teachers to become familiar with different ways of seeing the world. In fact, even "success" is defined differently by different cultures. Only by understanding *why* people behave and think as they do can a teacher hope to make real connections with students and their parents. Authentic cross-cultural connections, based not just on tolerance but on understanding and appreciation, are essential if students and their parents are to feel they are part of the school. We know what happens when students and families do not feel as though they belong: less parent involvement, lower student achievement, and higher drop-out rates.

We speak here of "cross-cultural" connections because it is relatively rare that Latino, African-American, or Vietnamese students (and others from nondominant communities) actually have teachers whose backgrounds match theirs. Approximately 13.5% of teachers in U.S. schools are non-White, while 34.4% of students are (U.S. Department of Commerce, U.S. Bureau of the Census, 1998). With current trends, the imbalance of representation of "minorities" in the teaching population will not be addressed in the foreseeable future.

Latino students (called "Hispanic" in the census literature) constitute 14.3% of the total student population — and vastly greater percentages in several states (U.S. Department of Commerce, U.S. Bureau of the Census, 1999). But only 4.2% of teachers nationwide are identified as Hispanic. The discrepancies are doubtless magnified in states like California, with 38% of its five and a half million students identified as Hispanic and New Mexico with 46.4%. African-American or "Black" students constitute 16.7% of the population (with greatly higher percentages in several states and urban areas), yet only 7.4% of teachers are reported as Black. "Asian and Pacific Island" students make up 3.6% of the population, but only 1.1% of teachers are described as such. American Indian and Alaska Native students are about 1.1% of the total U.S. population, while 0.8% of teachers are from those groups. (We use quotation marks around many of these categories because students' identities are no doubt often more complex than the nomenclature would suggest.)

These statistics underscore the point that teaching students from ethnic backgrounds different from one's own is the norm rather than the exception for a great many teachers. Therefore, anything that can help them to become aware of their own culture and the cultures of others is worth examining. But ethnicity is not the same as culture. Even teachers from the same ethnic background as their students can benefit from "cross-cultural" training. Sometimes, for example, the educational process required to become a teacher separates teachers from the home culture of their students, which they may originally have shared. Formal education in U.S. schools tends to cause teachers to subordinate their own cultural knowledge to the expectations of the dominant culture.

INTRODUCING A FRAMEWORK
FOR UNDERSTANDING CULTURE

This *Guide* offers a framework for understanding differences between the values of cultures based to a greater degree on "individualism" and those based to a greater degree on "collectivism" (Hofstede, 1983; Triandis, 1989). This framework is helpful for teachers who work with Latino (and other) immigrant children who are forced to move daily between a more collectivistic value system at home and the more individualistic value system of the dominant culture represented in school. Teachers who understand that value systems explain the "why" of any culture's important beliefs and behaviors have a powerful way of understanding their students and their students' families. Teachers have found that by using the *Bridging Cultures* framework, they are able to generate their own solutions to problems, develop methods for effective teaching, and work with parents as true partners.

The *Bridging Cultures* framework helps make teaching easier because teachers are working with, not against, the cultural values and practices children bring from home. For this reason, the framework also helps teachers, schools, and parents prevent cross-cultural conflicts of both a covert and overt nature.

In this *Guide*, we will share what the researchers and teachers of the *Bridging Cultures Project* have learned about how to develop cross-cultural understanding and apply it to improving home-school relationships with their students' immigrant Latino parents. It is important to note that in this book the focus is on immigrant Latino families because this is the primary population with which the *Bridging Cultures* framework was used. However, the framework can be used as well by teachers working with other immigrant groups. We will offer examples along the way from other cultures in order to suggest how the framework and methods we propose might be useful in learning about and working with students and families from other backgrounds.

The *Guide* is one of several publications arising from the *Bridging Cultures Project*. It is not a "how-to" handbook, although we do offer teachers specific suggestions on how to improve home-school relationships with immigrant Latino families and others. Instead, *Bridging Cultures* is a generative paradigm from which a virtually infinite number of innovative practices can be created by teachers working within the framework. Thus, the specific examples presented in the *Guide* are not recipes to follow but practices that teachers trained in the *Bridging Cultures* framework have generated out of this paradigm. We hope the *Guide* will stimulate broad thinking about how to meet the challenges of education in a pluralistic society — a society made up of people from many different cultural, linguistic, and ethnic backgrounds. Again, although the research underlying *Bridging Cultures* and the *Guide* focuses on immigrant Latino families, we believe the framework is a potent tool for learning about other cultures. It turns out that many other cultural groups face similar discrepancies between their own approaches to child-rearing and schooling and the approach of the dominant culture.

A TRULY *USEFUL* THEORETICAL FRAMEWORK

No prescription can be written for the complex decision-making teachers must engage in every day, as they seek to support educational equity for every student and as they attempt to understand how the cultures of home and school can best be brought together. However, some theoretical frameworks can give us practical insight into human behavior by helping us understand how it is rooted in particular cultural values. This is especially true of the framework we've worked with in *Bridging Cultures*, and we are eager to share what we are learning, so our fellow educators can use it to develop creative solutions to the challenges of cultural diversity in their own situations.

Because we want to get beyond prescriptions to deeper understanding, we focus more on the "whys" than the "how-tos" of the actions we propose. Teachers often intuitively use strategies that have merit, but if they don't have a good rationale for using them, they may jettison them after a time. As one *Bridging Cultures* teacher observed, "I am more likely to perpetuate certain practices now, because I have a reason to perpetuate them. I understand why they work, and I am teaching with more awareness, more mindfulness." At the same time, the framework allows us to focus on broad concepts rather than specific details about specific cultures. We agree with cross-cultural psychologist Richard Brislin that in learning about culture, it is more useful to "aim at concepts that *underlie* specific differences" (Brislin, 1993). Before we go any further, we must also acknowledge that *any* framework is only a tool to generate thoughtful questions and intelligent observation. Generalizations about any culture or group always bring with them the risk of oversimplifying the immense complexity of human life. So we caution readers to resist the temptation to use the tool we present here to jump to conclusions about any group or any individual.

THE *BRIDGING CULTURES* PROJECT

We want also to introduce readers to *Bridging Cultures* itself, the project that has brought staff researchers and teacher researchers together in such synergy and that is now producing a range of professional development materials and activities. The choice of the bridge metaphor in our project's name reflects the recognition that both cultures (the culture of home and the culture of school) are important: Our strategies seek to help people use the bridge to travel back and forth between the two orientations. At times, a "cross-cultural traveler" may just want to perch in the middle of the bridge and survey what lies beyond either end. With knowledge of the territory extending beyond the bridge on either side, a person has greater perspective and hence greater opportunity for conscious choices in thought and action. So, our working model of what makes for student success is a "bicultural" one — meaning that both students and teachers must acquire elements of each other's culture.

Bridging Cultures is a collaborative research and development project among educational researchers at WestEd (a regional educational laboratory); University of California, Los Angeles (UCLA); California State University at Northridge; and seven elementary teachers from six public schools in three school districts in Southern California. The ultimate goal of the project is to help teachers teach their students from diverse backgrounds with greater success. This group has been working together since the fall of 1996, when teachers were first introduced to the framework of individualism / collectivism through a series of three professional development workshops conducted by the other members of the team.

Teachers as Researchers

A key feature of the project is the role teachers take. The seven participating teachers are themselves acting as researchers in their own classrooms and contributing both to a deeper understanding of the theoretical framework and to the collection of examples of school-based experiences and practices that bring the framework alive. (These examples should also be useful to other teachers as they think about how to modify their own practices.) They are truly "teacher-researchers" because they experiment with new ways of bridging cultures, and they report the results for others to learn from. We refer to ourselves (the authors) as "staff researchers." Others have used the terms "inside researchers" to refer to teachers and "outside researchers" to refer to those not directly involved in the schools (cf., Cochran-Smith & Lytle, 1993).

    All of us are, in actuality, both teachers and researchers. To use Eleanor Duckworth's definition of teacher, each of us is "someone who engages learners, who seeks to involve each person wholly — mind, sense of self, sense of humor, range of interests, interactions with other people — in learning" (Duckworth, 1987, p. 134). A simple definition of researcher — whether classroom teacher or university professor — is "one who engages in 'intentional systematic inquiry' " (Dinkelman, 1997, p. 250). We believe that teacher research is an important and unique source of knowledge about teaching and that the artificial boundaries between teaching and research on teaching need to be challenged.

Practical Ways to Improve Home-School Relationships

In the *Guide*, we discuss ways to improve home-school relationships (and thus parent and family involvement) that are based on the experimentation of the teacher-researchers in their own classrooms as well as on other research. We make specific suggestions for:

- understanding differences between home cultures and school culture
- enhancing cross-cultural communication
- organizing parent-teacher conferences that work

- using strategies that increase parent involvement in schooling
- supporting teachers to become researchers
- using ethnographic techniques to learn about home cultures

ORGANIZATION OF THE *GUIDE*

In Chapter 1, the *Bridging Cultures* framework of individualism and collectivism is fully explained and illustrated through concrete examples. Although the chapters do not have to be read in order, this chapter should probably be read first to ground the reader in the meaning of the rest of the book. Chapter 2 discusses how schools have typically tried to involve parents and why some of the traditional strategies may not work with parents from non-dominant communities. We suggest alternatives to traditional practice that have proven more successful with Latino immigrant parents who have had little chance for formal education. Because of the importance and universality of parent-teacher conferences as a home-school link, we have devoted a whole chapter to them (Chapter 3). We examine what can go wrong in cross-cultural parent-teacher conferences and recommend strategies for improving them through better communication based on understanding of culture. The focus of Chapter 4 is on finding common ground across home and school cultures in order to engage both students and their parents. The suggestions in Chapters 3 and 4 arise from *Bridging Cultures* teacher-researchers' classroom experiences and experimentation, from the research of Patricia Greenfield and her colleagues at UCLA, and from other literature on culture and schooling.

Chapter 5 deals with the teacher as researcher, exploring the tradition of action research in education and offering illustrations from our experience with *Bridging Cultures* and from other action research projects. Ethnography as a research tool is introduced here. We believe that teachers need to conduct their own ethnographic research to find out how their students' cultures approach the roles of parents and teachers, the role of schooling, and expectations about children's behavior (some of the areas of cultural variation explored in the *Guide*). We close with a very short chapter (Chapter 6) that is a reflection on what has been most informative and most inspiring about the project.

Appendix A describes the *Bridging Cultures Project* in greater detail. The reader will learn more about the participants, the professional development workshops, and the project's impact on teachers.

A FEW WORDS ABOUT TERMINOLOGY

In this *Guide*, we use the terms "European-American," "African-American," and "Latino/a," for example, to characterize individuals and groups of people. (Each of these terms, of course, can refer to people from many nations and many social and historical backgrounds.) We use these rather than racial or ethnic terms, such as "Black," "White," or "Brown" because we are focusing on *cultural* values and attributes and not race or ethnicity. Culture may *cross* races and ethnicities. For example, Latino immigrants and Korean immigrants have much in common cultur-ally, while differing in ethnicity as well as history, language, and other attributes. African-Americans share certain values with these two groups, but they have a significant overlap in values with European-Americans as well. We do not intend to deny in any way the impact of race on people living in the United States — or elsewhere, for that matter. Racism, one of the excesses to which ethnic pride can become subject, is certainly an ongoing problem in our society. We believe a cultural analysis complements a race-based analysis of conflicts experienced by students in our schools. Using culture as a basis for understanding human differ-ences and commonalities has been shown in our work to lead to very positive changes in human relationships and in the quality of schooling.

The term "mainstream" carries the implication that one group of people or set of values is more central or acceptable. Yet, it is a convenient shorthand for what most would understand to mean "those who share a set of values that are normative in major societal institutions such as schools and government," and we use it on occasion for that reason. We also use the term "dominant" to refer to this same group because their values do dominate in many contexts. We should point out, also, that the dominant culture effectively includes members of ethnic minori-ties who have acquired dominant culture values, often through the process of schooling. The term "minority," although numerically accurate when used to refer to many groups, also has unfortunate connotations of "lesser" or "less impor-tant." It could be argued that this connotation accurately reflects the status of these groups in the society. Of course, Latinos or "Hispanics," as they are called in census data, may not be a numerical minority for many more decades (nor are they in many classrooms), a fact that leads to questions about how they should be characterized. "Majority-minority" is one rather unsatisfying response. For the reasons outlined here, we have attempted to use specific terms (Mexican-Ameri-can, Korean-American, Navajo, or Yup'ik) whenever possible. When we do use the term "minority," we put it in quotation marks to indicate its limitations.

ACKNOWLEDGMENTS

The heart of the *Bridging Cultures Project* has been its participating teachers, who are named at the very outset of this book. We can hardly acknowledge their contributions enough. We wish to thank their cooperating schools and administrators, as well, for supporting the teachers by allowing them to try various innovations within their classrooms and to share what they have learned with their school faculties.

The project has been supported financially in large part by the Office of Educational Research and Improvement, through its grant to WestEd, the regional laboratory for the western region of the country, which is based in San Francisco and can be found at http://web.wested.org.

Dr. Carrie Rothstein-Fisch's participation has been partially underwritten by a small grant from the College of Education at California State University, Northridge, allowing her time for classroom observations and intensive interviews of the teacher-researchers.

We owe thanks to Dr. Sharon Nelson-Barber, Director of the Culture and Language in Education Program at WestEd, who is an expert on cultural issues in teacher education and has shared her own insights with us all along the way. We also thank current and former WestEd staff members, particularly Rosemarie Garcia Fontana, Joy Zimmerman, and Jim Johnson who read early drafts of the book and offered immensely helpful suggestions. Rebeca Diaz-Meza, who recently joined the *Bridging Cultures Project* as a Research Associate at WestEd, has contributed important insights to the parent involvement issue, both from the perspective of her own personal experience and on the basis of her dissertation research with Latina parents involved in their children's schooling. Aida Hasan, a research intern during the final stages of writing the book, deserves thanks for tracking down wayward references and responding with whatever support was requested of her.

Thanks go to the Center for the Study of Evolution and Origin of Life at UCLA for hosting our *Bridging Cultures* workshops in its library over a period of years. We also appreciate the help of German Hercules, Annie Tsai, and Nick Breitborde in organizing our *Bridging Cultures* workshop meetings and providing other support.

We extend many thanks to Naomi Silverman, our editor, who immediately recognized value in our manuscript and helped us develop it into a resource we can all be proud of. Finally, much appreciation goes to Cherry Elliott, who prepared the camera-ready manuscript.

chapter 1

The *Bridging Cultures* Framework

BUT FIRST, WHAT IS CULTURE?

One definition of culture emphasizes its arts, artifacts, traditional dress, culinary practices, rituals and ceremonies, and norms of social interaction. It is focused on material elements and observable patterns of behavior and customs (Fetterman, 1988; Hollins, 1996). Another approach to defining culture is to focus on its "ideational" aspect: the ideas, beliefs, knowledge of groups — what might be called a "cognitive" approach (Fetterman, 1988, p. 27). In a way, it is quite artificial to separate these two; undoubtedly they are intimately related. Our orientation to culture incorporates both realms but is primarily focused on the ideational elements: ideas, beliefs, knowledge, and ways of acquiring knowledge and passing it on (learning and teaching). Not only do individuals and groups have cultures, institutions do as well. At times we speak of "school culture" or "the culture of schooling." These terms are justified because when one looks at school districts across the country, one sees a remarkable uniformity of values and practices (Hollins, 1996). This uniformity ignores the multiplicity of student cultures and variations in family approaches to learning, teaching, and child-rearing. It is as though only one culture, the dominant one — or the culture of those "in charge" — counts. In fact, the norms of schools are nearly always those of the larger society. In this respect, the school could be described as the acculturating agent.

1

We are exploring with teachers the ways in which deep value orientations of cultures (including the dominant U.S. culture) result in different expectations of children and of schooling. These orientations are less visible than the material elements of a culture or the ways a culture celebrates holidays, observes religious beliefs, or creates works of art. They are more difficult to capture than the histories of groups. Yet they form the basis for ways of viewing the world and vast ranges of behaviors, including the ways people communicate, discipline their children, and carry out everyday tasks. If schools are to succeed in promoting meaningful parent involvement, they need to understand how these orientations shape a whole host of beliefs, expectations, and behaviors — on the part of parents on the one hand, and of teachers and school personnel on the other.

THE POWER OF THE
BRIDGING CULTURES FRAMEWORK

We believe that a framework characterizing the features of individualism and collectivism is both *economical* and *generative*. It is economical because it incorporates and explains the relationship among many elements that have previously been regarded as separate, such as conceptions of schooling and education, attitudes toward family, expectations for role maintenance or flexibility (including sex roles), duties toward elders, authority structures, attitudes toward discipline, ways of dealing with property, and many aspects of communication. The framework is generative because it suggests interpretations of and explanations for an endless set of interactions among students in a classroom, between teacher and student(s), between teacher and parents, and between school and community.

In this *Guide*, our focus is on communication and relations between teacher and parents and between school and community. Examples from the teacher-researchers of the *Bridging Cultures Project* illustrate how the framework has guided teachers' thinking and action and generated reflection, mindfulness, and deeper understanding of culture-based issues in schooling. In fact, it was the teacher-researchers who urged development of this *Guide*. They hoped it would be a resource they could use with fellow teachers in their own schools and beyond.

LIMITATIONS OF A SINGLE MODEL
FOR CHILD DEVELOPMENT

The U.S. represents a confluence of voluntary immigrants, involuntary immigrants, and indigenous peoples — each with its own cultural history and roots. Groups have different approaches to child rearing, different norms of social behavior and communication, and different approaches to learning (Greenfield, 1994). Yet, teachers' understanding of how children develop, learn, and communicate is shaped primarily by a European-American model that represents what is normal for only one segment of their students. As mentioned earlier, this is true even for teachers who come from nondominant cultures, but who have been schooled in a European-American style educational system (Raeff, Greenfield, & Quiroz, 2000). To succeed in our schools, one has to become quite individualistic.

Teachers' expectations can lead students to feel as though they do or do not belong in the classroom, affecting their engagement in learning and, consequently, their achievement. Likewise, parents can come to feel at home in or alienated from their children's schools depending on the ways in which the school and its personnel interact with them. If schools are to engender and sustain real parent involvement, they will need frameworks for understanding cultural differences and strategies for actively bridging those differences.

The most well-meaning efforts to provide multicultural education or involve parents from nondominant cultures often fall far short of their aims. It has been observed that "[i]ronically, teachers may conscientiously try to create culturally sensitive environments for their students (e.g., through multicultural displays and activities), while simultaneously structuring classroom interaction patterns that violate invisible cultural norms of various nondominant groups. Teachers may also inadvertently criticize parents for adhering to a different set of ideals about children, families, and parenting" (Greenfield, Raeff & Quiroz, 1996, p. 40). These are unfortunate and unintended outcomes for all concerned.

THE DYNAMIC NATURE OF CULTURE

We must emphasize that there are elements of both individualism and collectivism in any society and that cultures change, particularly when they come in contact with each other. As Goldenberg and Gallimore observe, "Both continuity and discontinuity across generations are part of the process of cultural evolution, a complex dynamic that contributes to change and variability within cultures" (1995, p. 188). For example, parents' views about appropriate education for girls of the current generation of Mexican-American families are different from *their parents'* views on the same topic (Goldenberg & Gallimore, 1995; Greenfield, Raeff, & Quiroz, 1996).

While these rubrics or categories can be useful in helping us understand tendencies within a group, they should not lead to rigid predictions about specific beliefs of groups or individuals. It is important to recognize that even for immigrant Latino families, values and practices will vary based on the length of time they have been in the U.S., the level of education they attained in their countries of origin, how much time has been spent in an urban setting, and numerous other factors. The varying circumstances of immigrant Latino families lead to different ways of intersecting with the "mainstream" culture, and children's particular experiences in schools and in their communities affect the ways they will adapt to new cultural influences. Beyond all of this, cultures change over time on the basis of changes in their circumstances. For instance, there is strong evidence to suggest that as they become more economically advanced, cultures become more individualistic (Lustig & Koester, 1999).

We are certainly aware of the risks of positing any sort of categories into which human beings or their cultures can be sorted. Categories can be used to stereotype. But we agree with Hollins's (1996) assertion that "the publication of standardized test scores and other measures of academic achievement revealing discrepancies in performance based on race and ethnicity are more likely to lead to harmful stereotyping than appropriate adjustments to instruction that incorporate aspects of these students' home culture. The latter is more likely to improve the performance of underserved populations than maintaining existing approaches because of concern for misunderstanding and misinterpretations" (Hollins, 1996, p. 5). Others have, of course, struggled with the same dilemma. A researcher working with a group of teachers engaged in cultural research said, "…we worried *both* about stereotyping children — reducing complex individuals to simplistic examples of one kind of difference — *and* [emphasis added] about being ignorant of the particular home cultures and socioeconomic circumstances of the particular children in each school" (Dyson, with the San Francisco East Bay Teacher Study Group, p. 10). If we can remember that the framework is just a tool, a heuristic for helping us organize our observations and questions, we can avoid the pitfalls associated with categories.

INDIVIDUALISM AND COLLECTIVISM

The continuum of individualism / collectivism represents the degree to which a culture emphasizes individual fulfillment and choice versus interdependent relations, social responsibility, and the well-being of the group. Individualism makes the former a priority, collectivism the latter. Although the dominant U.S. culture is extremely individualistic, many immigrant cultures are strongly collectivistic, as are American Indian and Alaska Native cultures. African-American culture has been described as more collectivistic than the dominant culture, more oriented toward extended family and kinship-help patterns but still stressing the importance of individual achievement (Hill, 1972; McAdoo, 1978, cited in Hollins, 1996).

According to Blake (1994, p. 189), "The traditional cultural emphases of African Americans include interdependence, extended family, and personal expression. Generally, these values are discussed from the group's perspective, with major regard given to the importance of the collective 'us.' However, the 'us' is only one side of the proverbial coin, the other side being what Abrahams (1970) described as 'the constant consideration of the importance of the "me element" in Black life.' " These researchers suggest that African-Americans as a group are more collectivistic than members of the dominant culture but exhibit some of the prominent values of individualism as well.

About 70% of the world's cultures could be described as collectivistic (Triandis, 1989). At the most basic level, the difference is one of emphasis on individual success versus successful relations with others in a group. It could be characterized as the difference between "standing out" and "fitting in." In collectivistic cultures, people are more likely to identify their own personal goals with those of the group — extended family, religion, or other valued group (Brislin, 1993). When asked to complete the statement, "I am...." collectivists are more likely to respond with reference to an organization, family, or religion. Individualists tend to list trait labels referring to aspects of their personalities, such as "hardworking," "intelligent," or "athletic" (Triandis, Brislin, & Hui, 1988). The situation below illustrates the group orientation common to collectivistic cultures.

A VISIT TO THE PSYCHIATRIST

A Nigerian psychiatrist [reported] that when a psychiatric clinic was first set up in a rural district of Nigeria to treat the mentally ill, the family invariably accompanied the sufferer and insisted upon being present at the patient's interview with the psychiatrist. The idea that the patient might exist as an individual apart from the family, or that he might have personal problems which he did not want to share with them, did not occur to Nigerians who were still living a traditional village life (Storr, 1988, p. 78).

At the other extreme, not only do many North Americans go to psychiatrists privately for individual therapy, but they are also likely to be routinely counseled to "separate" from their families in order to have healthy adult lives. When immigrants from collectivistic societies find themselves in conflict with U.S. norms of individualism that promote this "healthy separation" from family and seek counseling, they can expect the same sort of advice — despite its lack of harmony with their own basic values.

These two orientations of individualism and collectivism guide rather different developmental scripts for children and for schooling; and conflicts between them are reflected daily in U.S. classrooms. Keener awareness of how they shape goals and behaviors can enable teachers and parents to interpret each other's expectations better and work together more harmoniously on behalf of students.

Documenting Different Orientations

Two of us (Greenfield and Quiroz), along with Catherine Raeff, began to document how different cultural values might lead to different strategies for dealing with social situations (Greenfield, Quiroz, & Raeff, 2000; Raeff, Greenfield, & Quiroz, 2000). In one study (Greenfield, Quiroz, & Raeff, 2000), parents, teachers, and fifth-grade students from two Los Angeles schools were asked to resolve conflicts presented in home- and school-based scenarios. The "Jobs Scenario" is an example.

THE JOBS SCENARIO:
SOLVING A CLASSROOM DILEMMA

It is the end of the school day, and the class is cleaning up. Salvador isn't feeling well, and he asks Emanuel to help him with his job for the day, which is cleaning the blackboard. Emanuel isn't sure that he will have time to do both jobs. What do you think the teacher should do?

Example of an *individualistic* response:

The teacher should find a third person to do Salvador's job. Emanuel has his own job and should not be bothered with another job.

Example of a *collectivistic* response:

The teacher should tell Emanuel to help Salvador with his job.

Ways of solving the dilemmas presented in the scenarios differed greatly from school to school (Figures 1.1 and 1.2). School 1 represents a primarily European-American population. The parents and children represented in Figure 1.1 were all European-American; the teachers were of mixed ethnicity. The dominant response in this school was that the teacher should find a third person, often a volunteer, to do Salvador's job. In fact, European-American parents, their children, and their children's teachers preferred this solution to the dilemma. Participants who gave this response tended to reason that Emanuel has his own job to do, and he should not be bothered with another job that would interfere with it. This response illustrates the value of not infringing on others' rights. It also reflects the value of protecting the individual's task assignment — one person, one task (Raeff, Greenfield, & Quiroz, 2000). Reference to a volunteer reflected the value placed on helping as a matter of individual choice. This kind of response represents the cultural value of individualism. Thus, for the European-American school population, there is broad agreement among parents, students, and school personnel around the value of individualism.

Figure 1.1
Dominant responses to "Jobs Scenario"
School 1 (European-American)

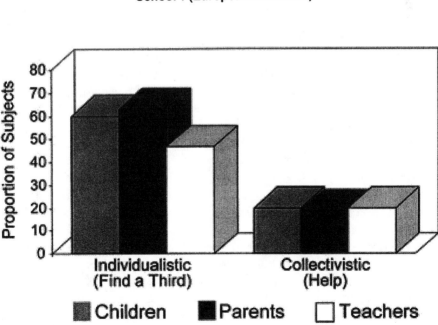

Figure 1.2
Dominant responses to "Jobs Scenario"
School 2 (Latino)

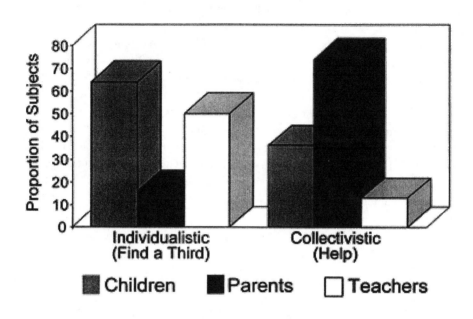

School 2 serves predominantly immigrant Latino populations. Again, the teachers are of mixed ethnicity. Immigrant Latino parents' responses (Fig.1.2) to the Jobs Scenario indicated that Emanuel's helping Salvador was the preferred way to solve the dilemma. Nearly three-quarters of the parents opted for this solution, reflecting the assumption that human beings are responsible for helping in-group members in order to contribute to the unity and welfare of the group. Responses of this kind reflect the cultural value of collectivism. In contrast, teachers in School 2 responded much like the teachers in School 1, and so did 64% of students. However, more students than in the European-American population (36% compared to 20%) recommended that Emanual help Salvador. In effect, most students solved the dilemma as their teachers did, while a substantial minority followed the preferred path of their parents.

Here we see that a simple dilemma regarding classroom jobs can reveal two different views of human development and social relationships. The harmony among different constituencies (parents, children, teachers) in School 1 is quite evident from a glance at the graph: most parents, teachers, and children had similar responses. In School 2, by contrast, one can see conflicting views among parents, teachers, and children. Most parents think the dilemma should be resolved in a collectivistic manner, whereas teachers favor the individualistic pathway. These differences between parents and teachers imply that the children are being socialized in conflicting manners at home and at school. They are being exposed to two different sets of cultural values, the collectivistic cultural values of home and the individualistic cultural values of school.

FURTHER CONTRASTS BETWEEN INDIVIDUALISM AND COLLECTIVISM

Treatment of the Physical World

Children socialized in an individualistic orientation are attuned early on to learning about physical objects and the physical world as a way of facilitating independence (Quiroz & Greenfield, 1996; Greenfield & Suzuki, 1998). Parents often encourage children to amuse themselves with toys, so that they will be independent and not require constant adult attention. Learning how to manipulate toys is also the beginning of what might be called "technological intelligence," something highly valued in individualistic societies (Mundy-Castle, 1974). Parents tend to use language as opposed to physical interaction to communicate with children and to control their behavior. It would not be unusual to see a child playing with her toys in a playpen or crawling around the floor while Mom or Dad talks to her at a distance. This approach is in contrast to what happens with children socialized in a collectivistic orientation, where the value of physical objects is primarily that they mediate social relationships in the way that gifts do (Greenfield, Brazelton, & Childs, 1989). Holding, touching, and modeling how to carry out a task (rather than direct oral language) tend to be the dominant form of communication between parent and child (Greenfield, 1994).

A poignant example of the culturally different ways of regarding objects comes from observations of classroom discussions. In one instance, a kindergarten teacher was showing her class an actual chicken egg that would be hatching soon. She asked the children to describe eggs by thinking about the times they had cooked and eaten them. An immigrant Latina child tried three times to talk about a morning when she and her grandmother had cooked eggs together. But the teacher disregarded her comments in favor of a child who explained how eggs look white and yellow when they are cracked (Greenfield, Raeff, & Quiroz, 1996). The teacher wanted the children to focus strictly on the physical properties of eggs and not their social meaning, but the child was not aware of this expectation. What's more, the teacher's question was actually ambiguous. She had explicitly requested that the children think about times they had cooked and eaten eggs. What she did not make explicit was her expectation that children talk about the physical but not the social aspects of these occasions.

In classrooms, we often ask students to discuss objects (and concepts or facts) as things in themselves, apart from any social context or meaning they might have. Such an orientation to objects is unfamiliar to many students, whether they are immigrant Latino, American Indian, Pacific Islander, or from another group that has a collectivistic value system. The teacher in the egg example was unaware that her question was ambiguous. Children who shared the teacher's value orientation would assume that she was interested in the physical properties of the eggs, although she had not made this point explicit. However, those children who did not share the teacher's value orientation would likely make different assumptions. They would almost certainly assume that she was interested in the object as a mediator of social relationships.

Treatment of Property

The emphasis on social relationships rather than on the individual extends to notions of property: in collectivistic cultures, the boundaries of property ownership are more permeable. Personal items such as clothing, books, or toys are readily shared and often seen as family property rather than individual property (see "The Crayons Incident").

THE CRAYONS INCIDENT

A mentor teacher paid a visit to a kindergarten class, where she observed that the teacher had arranged the crayons by color in cups. There was a cup for the green crayons, a cup for the red crayons, and so on. Each cup of crayons was shared by the entire class. The mentor suggested to the kindergarten teacher that it would be much better if each child had his or her own cup of crayons with all of the colors in it. She explained that it made children feel good to have their own property and that they needed to learn how to take care of their own property. Furthermore, those who took good care of their "property" would not have to suffer by using the "crappy" (her word) crayons of those children who did not know how to take care of their things (Quiroz & Greenfield, 1996).

Interpretation of "The Crayons Incident"

The crayons incident involves an underlying conflict between the values of sharing and personal property. The kindergarten teacher was an immigrant Latina parent herself, and her arrangement of the crayons was implicitly based on her collectivistic orientation. When she responded to the wishes of the supervising teacher by rearranging the crayons, the children, largely immigrant Latinos themselves, began to experience conflict between the sharing orientation that was familiar to them at home (and previously in school) and the new orientation to personal property. The children "did not care if their materials were misplaced, so their 'personal' materials ended up having to be rearranged by the teacher every day. It was not that the children were incapable of arranging their materials in a systematic fashion, because they had done so before. However, the category 'personal material' simply was not important to them" (Quiroz & Greenfield, 1996, pp. 12-13).

Sources of Knowledge

In a collectivistic value system, it is considered disrespectful for children to communicate their opinions to older people. Therefore, children in collectivistic cultures are not likely to be asked to formulate and share their views with others or verbalize about what they are learning (as they will be expected to do in school). The role of sharing opinions or knowledge is reserved for people with higher status. Hierarchical relationships and respect for elders and authority keep people in their appropriate roles — roles that are necessary to the continuity and stability of the cultural community (Kim & Choi, 1994; Suina & Smolkin, 1994; Triandis, 1989). For example, in many American Indian cultures, designated heirs are in charge of particular knowledge. The eldest son or nephew of a spiritual leader may be taught certain knowledge that only he is allowed to possess and pass on.[1]

Another contrast between the two orientations is that although elders are the source of knowledge and wisdom in collectivistic communities, not only the teacher but also impersonal texts are the authoritative sources in the individualis-

---

[1] Role hierarchy and stability do not mean that younger people cannot take leadership, exert autonomy, or assume considerable responsibility. To the contrary, children in collectivistic cultures often have the responsibility of caring for younger siblings and carrying out important household tasks. In subsistence societies (such as Alaska Native and some American Indian), children are expected to learn many skills at a young age and make decisions about when they feel competent to perform them, with possible survival consequences for other members of their group (Au & Kawakami, 1994; Nelson-Barber & Dull, 1998).

tic classroom (Greenfield, 1994). In addition, children themselves are free to consult texts and build their own knowledge.

One can see how a more socially-grounded concept of being well-educated ("*bien educado*," in Spanish) would grow out of the collectivistic orientation (Goldenberg & Gallimore, 1995). From such a point of view, cognitive development in itself is not the main goal of development, or at least it is not seen as a goal in itself apart from development that characterizes a good human being in that context. By contrast, the egalitarian, individualistic "mainstream" society encourages children to become independent thinkers and doers who focus on their own intellectual achievement (see "Cognitive versus Social Skills," pp. 17-18).

Source of the "Self"

Many European-Americans believe that the self is "located solely within the individual and the individual is definitely separate from others. From a very young age, children are encouraged to make their own decisions" (Lustig & Koester, 1999, p. 95). They are expected to learn to maintain strong borders between the self and others. But a child reared in a collectivistic community is socialized to have his or her sense of self based on affiliation with the group (principally the family) and responsibility to the other members of the group, rather than on personal achievement for his or her own ends. There is less psychological or emotional distance from other people, and "the collective becomes the place in which people find their identity as human beings" (Brislin, 1993, p. 49). In Korean culture (as in the cultures of immigrant Latino families), it is group membership that largely defines the self. One reflection of this orientation is seen in people's perceptions and use of the personal pronoun "we" ("*woori*"). *Woori* is used in many cases where a European-American would use "I." The pronoun also connotes an affective bond with the other members of one's group and unity or oneness of the group — more so than the pronoun "we" connotes in the dominant U.S. culture (Choi, Kim, & Choi, 1993).

Other Differences: Implications for Schooling

Perhaps the most obvious differences between the individualistic and the collectivistic orientations seen in the classroom have to do with the degree of emphasis on independence, individual achievement, self-expression, and personal choice. The ways people (teacher and students) interact in the classroom reflect a relative emphasis on the needs of the group or of the individual. Competition is the natural companion of a focus on the individual, while the natural companion of a focus on the group is cooperation. Although "cooperative learning" has been widely promoted, sometimes on the grounds that it will improve students' later success on the job, the norm of cooperation has clearly not overridden the norm of competition. The conflict between the two norms is seen most clearly in settings such as Southern California, where immigrant Latinos are introduced to U.S. schooling, or Alaska, where students from indigenous cultures meet "mainstream" teaching. Yup'ik Eskimo teacher Vicki Dull explains the situation in the village where she taught: "… in Yup'ik culture the 'group' is important. There is little, if any, competition among Yup'ik people. When the Western school system entered the picture, the unity of the group slowly shattered. Children were sent hundreds and often thousands of miles away to be schooled in boarding schools where they were forced to abandon their own language for the foreign English with its accompanying foreign ways. They learned the Western value of competition. They learned to be individuals competing against each other instead of a group working in unity. …There were seldom, if any times when they were allowed to help each other, which would have been construed as 'cheating' " (Dull, in Nelson-Barber & Dull, 1998, p. 95). It is difficult for educators used to U.S. "mainstream" norms to comprehend how drastic a shift this represents for students from a collectivistic culture.

DIFFERENT ORIENTATIONS, DIFFERENT OUTCOMES

It does not take much to imagine how these substantially different orientations would prepare children quite differently for schooling, as well as how parents from these different orientations would have distinct ideas about what a school should be like. More collectivistic parents might envision a classroom where children show respect for others and for learning by quiet listening; where concern for everyone's success is manifest in a great deal of mutual helping; and where social skills are nurtured as much as academic skills. More individualistic parents might hope for an active learning environment where children are supported to develop their own knowledge and opinions; where children are responsible for their own property and performance; and where the greater emphasis is on academic achievement, with some attention to social skills. The two orientations also typically lead to different patterns of classroom organization. While collectivistic cultures tend to teach to the whole group or allow students to learn from each other (peer-oriented learning), individualistic ones tend to focus on the individual and emphasize individual responsibility for learning (cf., Estrin & Nelson-Barber, 1995; Stigler & Perry, 1988).

INDIVIDUALISM AND COLLECTIVISM IN COLLISION

We have already presented examples of how these two different value orientations often collide as children from immigrant Latino families move from home culture into U.S. schools (Greenfield & Cocking, 1994; Greenfield, Raeff, & Quiroz, 1998; Raeff, Greenfield & Quiroz, 2000). Children of immigrant families may be torn between the values and expectations of their native culture and those of the "mainstream." Parents and teachers (the latter representing the "mainstream" culture) may observe the same behaviors in children but interpret them differently, because they are viewing them through very different cultural lenses. When the individualistic teacher says the child is "able to work well independently," the collectivistic parent may hear the teacher as saying the child is "too separated from the group." When the collectivistic parent asks more than once about his child's social development, the individualistic teacher may hear the parent as saying, "I don't really care whether she does well in school."

Sources of Home-School Conflict

The research of Greenfield and her colleagues on individualism and collectivism has identified several areas of potential conflict that teachers may observe in the classroom or in interactions with parents (see Greenfield, Quiroz, & Raeff, 2000; Raeff, Greenfield, & Quiroz, 2000; Greenfield, Raeff, & Quiroz, 1996; Quiroz & Greenfield, 1996). Table 1.1 (p. 16) summarizes these conflicts. Each is a manifestation of an underlying conflict between a more individualistic and a more collectivistic perspective. Each occurs when the collectivistic tradition of Latino (and likely many other) immigrant families encounters the individualistic tradition of U.S. schools.

The Individual versus the Group

Conflicts over focusing on the child as individual versus the child as group member take many forms. For example, during a parent conference, the teacher may assume that the child's achieving her potential for the sake of self-fulfillment is a valid goal of education (a more individualistic perspective). Her parents, on the other hand, may be far more concerned with how well their child is integrating into the group or how she contributes her efforts to the social whole (a collectivistic perspective). Of course, this does not mean parents do not value the child's achievement, but they want it to serve a social purpose. In the conference, the parents may (unconsciously) try to switch the focus from an *individual* child's achievement to the *family* constellation by bringing up how their other children are doing in school (Greenfield, Quiroz, & Raeff, 2000). Such a move is another instance of the inclination to consider the child's success in terms of the group rather than as an individual.

Bridging Cultures researchers documented an interesting case of cross-cultural conflict involving a federally-funded breakfast program in a public school (Greenfield, Raeff, & Quiroz, 1996). According to federal guidelines, only children enrolled in the school are permitted to eat these breakfasts. The problem was that immigrant Latina mothers were coming to school with their children and sharing the breakfasts with the family.

School officials saw this as a problem, not only because of the federal guidelines, but because they interpreted the behavior as "mothers taking food away from their children." So they shut the gates of the school and, with no explanation, stopped allowing parents in at breakfast time. A sign reading, "Only students allowed in the eating area" was posted. From the cultural perspective of the mothers, however, the family that comes to school to have breakfast with a child is demonstrating the value of sharing and contributing to the welfare of the whole family. Bringing the younger siblings to share in the breakfast is the mother's way of fulfilling her responsibility to the family as a whole. In fact, it may be almost inconceivable from such a cultural perspective to think of a family member — particularly a young child — eating without sharing with the rest of the family when it is possible to do otherwise. Values like these are so deep and unconscious that they go unquestioned, whether from the "mainstream" perspective or from another cultural perspective.

Independence versus Helpfulness

Teachers, who tend to be individualistic, may value highly a child's ability to work independently and to focus on getting his or her own work done (Raeff, Greenfield, & Quiroz, 2000). On the other hand, parents from a collectivistic orientation are likely to pay more attention to how helpful and cooperative their child is in the classroom. Helpfulness is also valued in our "mainstream" classroom culture, but it becomes a lower priority when it is seen to interfere with individual achievement and individual responsibility. At the limit, it is called "cheating." The teacher may be more concerned with the child's taking responsibility for his or her own work and for cleaning up his or her own materials. However, in collectivistic cultures, the priorities are different. A Latino parent may hope to see children helping each other complete both academic and housekeeping tasks, as in the classroom jobs scenario. Likewise, Japanese parents, on the whole, value kindness and helpful-

Table 1.1 Sources of Home-School Conflict

Individualism	*Collectivism*
Child as individual	Child as part of the group
Independence	Helpfulness
Praise (for positive self-esteem)	Criticize (for normative behavior)
Cognitive skills	Social skills
Oral expression	Listening to authority
Parents' role is to teach	Teacher's role is to educate
Personal property	Sharing

(Based on Quiroz & Greenfield, 1996.)

ness as key elements of their children's becoming good community members. They expect the primary school to devote considerable time daily to developing those traits in their children (Lewis, 1995).

Praise versus Criticism

Many immigrant Latino parents are not comfortable with hearing extended praise of their children (Greenfield, Quiroz, & Raeff, 2000). Praise singles a child out from the group, whereas criticism has a normative effect, bringing the child in line with the group. The teachers of *Bridging Cultures* have noted that the standard wisdom in most "mainstream" American schools is to "sandwich a small amount of criticism in-between a lot of praise." The rationale for this is to raise the child's self-esteem. Moles, for example, recommends that during the conference, the teacher "establish rapport with parents, accept parents as advocates, establish priorities, learn from the parents, and *emphasize the positive*" (1996, p. 22). He states that research shows parents are "more willing to listen to a range of feedback about their child if they hear the teacher comment on the child's special qualities first" (p. 22).

But this advice is not universally helpful, as we know. One of us (Quiroz), herself an immigrant Latina parent, has talked about her own discomfort with being praised in front of other students in her graduate courses. Similarly, when she goes to a parent-teacher conference about her fourth-grader, she wants to know what her daughter needs to work on. And she is greatly concerned with the child's overall social and moral development, not just academic achievement. In a parent conference, the parent who believes one of his or her most important tasks in child-rearing is to help shape the child's behavior to meet expectations will want to hear from the teacher what needs to be done to accomplish that task, too.

It is not only immigrant Latino parents who may be uncomfortable at times with praise of their children. This trait is shared by many parents from other collectivistic cultures. For example, Yup'ik Eskimo teacher Evelyn Yanez says that "overly praising is wrong because it can make one feel better than others and this could be particularly damaging in an interdependent society" (Lipka & Yanez, 1998, p. 132). In the context of a lesson on stringing smelt (a traditional Yup'ik practice), Yanez waits until toward the end of the lesson, praises children for doing well, and mentions how nice it will be that they can help their mother or grandmother string smelt later. Her praise is related to the importance of acquiring the cultural knowledge and helping the family. It is not for individual achievement as a goal in itself.

Cognitive versus Social Skills

Immigrant parents from collectivistic cultures may be more interested in social behaviors and social skills, while teachers tend to focus on the cognitive development of children. As discussed earlier, parents may see cognitive development as dependent on social or moral development. Goldenberg and Gallimore report on a study they did with immigrant parents from Mexico and Central America in which they sought parents' views about education (1995). They found that many parents did not distinguish between education as *schooling* and education as *upbringing*. The authors say that even when they urged parents to differentiate between the two, it was impossible for many. They saw them as inextricably linked. One father expressed a thought echoed by many others, "The two things [formal study and moral rectitude] go hand in hand.... It would be impossible to get to the university if one doesn't have good behavior, if one isn't taught to respect others..." (Goldenberg & Gallimore, 1995, p. 198).

Given the way in which immigrant Latino parents may conceptualize education, it is not surprising that a dominant (although not always welcome) theme these parents introduce into parent-teacher conferences is children's behavior. *Bridging Cultures* teachers note that one of the first questions a Latino immigrant parent will ask is, "*¿Como se porta mi hijo/a?*" ("How is my son/daughter behaving?") The teacher may try to direct the conversation toward the child's academic achievement, only to be asked again about the child's behavior. Teachers may encounter similar questions from Vietnamese-American or Japanese-American parents, who see moral and social development as essential to the education process (California Department of Education, 1994; Lewis, 1995).

Oral Expression versus Respect for Authority

Skillful self-expression, critical thinking, ability to engage in discussion and argument — these are all valued attributes of the "ideal student," according to many of the current educational reform efforts. However, parents may be unresponsive to or even negative about teachers' emphasis on oral self-expression. They may believe that a quiet student will learn more and is more respectful than one who speaks up, singling himself or herself out from the group and taking time away from the teacher's talk. So, when a teacher is talking at length in a parent-teacher conference about what a "critical thinker" the student is and how well he formulates questions, a parent may be alarmed rather than overjoyed. (See box below for an example of how this kind of conflict was resolved.)

**MAKING CULTURAL ASSUMPTIONS EXPLICIT:
AN EXAMPLE FROM THE PACIFIC**

In a related project with which the first author is involved, schools and communities in U.S. entities in Micronesia worked together to fashion mathematics and science standards that would be culturally-compatible (Pacific Mathematics and Science Leadership Team, 1995). While they subscribed to the view that the best learning is active learning and that students should be encouraged to ask questions and think critically, they wanted to preserve respect for elders and their wisdom. For this reason, they developed specific guidelines about when it is appropriate for children to ask questions and how the questions may be asked, depending on the setting. Elders' wisdom is meant to be listened to and pondered. And the child's ability to understand this wisdom increases over the course of a lifetime, as a result of his or her own experience. Interrogation of an elder is inappropriate. However, in the classroom it *is* appropriate to ask probing questions and to expect a teacher or fellow student to respond (even if only with an additional question). By making the two sets of values explicit, parents and teachers were able to make headway toward resolving a serious conflict.

The issue of authority is not a small one, and it has come up in many settings where European-American teachers are teaching "minority" students. Students may mistake a teacher's indirect methods of managing behavior or emphasis on self-control of behavior for weakness on the part of the teacher. The teacher implicitly believes such self-control is necessary for the development of independence and initiative. Parents may have the same response as students and wonder why the teacher is not simply telling the student in a more authoritative way what to do, what to think, or how to behave. But we must caution that not all teachers' authority looks the same, even across collectivistic cultures. For example, descriptions of teachers' behaviors and thinking in both Alaskan (Yup'ik Eskimo) and Japanese elementary schools reflect a friendly attitude, rather than directive or punitive, and a belief that children need to and are capable of learning how to manage their own behavior within a group (Nelson-Barber & Dull, 1998; Lewis, 1995). In these cases, support to control one's behavior also comes from the group. It is the group of peers and not the individual child that is the "unit of control."

A related issue is that students who are unaccustomed to being "information-givers" in their home interactions with adults may not be prepared for the rapid-fire question and answer sessions that take place in some classrooms. Teachers may mistakenly assume they do not have the information or understand the questions (Eggen & Kauchak, 1997; Heath, 1983).

Parents' Roles versus Teachers' Roles

The educational maxim "parents are children's first teachers" is true in many senses. But not all parents agree with the increasingly academic role they are being asked to take with their children. Teachers often suggest to parents that they work on specific academic skills at home. In the minds of many immigrant Latino parents, this is not the role they see as appropriate for themselves (Quiroz & Greenfield, 1996). They may believe academic instruction should be restricted to school and can be done better by the teacher. For example, research has shown that many immigrant Latinos residing in Los Angeles had (prior to immigration) six or fewer years of education from a country whose educational system is quite different from that of the U.S. They may not feel qualified to teach academics at home. They may, however, be interested in *learning* academic skills *with* their children (Greenfield, Quiroz & Raeff, unpublished data, 1995).

However, these same parents *do* want to maintain jurisdiction as socializing agents at home, and they probably *do not* want advice on parenting skills — something schools seem to hand out with increasing frequency. It is not surprising that these parents would resist parenting advice from the schools, given that teachers, with their individualistic value system, are working at cross purposes to the socializing influence of the home. Parents probably have expectations of teachers with which teachers may not feel entirely comfortable. The parallel expression to "parents are children's first teachers" in Spanish is "*la maestra es la segunda mamá*" ("the teacher is the child's second mother"). Parents are likely to expect that the teacher take a stronger role vis-à-vis the development of social and moral skills than the teacher has in mind. They may believe the school is remiss in not addressing this aspect of development adequately.

Personal Property versus Sharing

In many immigrant families from collectivist cultures, most possessions are shared. People use things when they need them, and one need not even ask permission to do so. Responsibility for caring for material goods is also shared (see "Independence versus helpfulness," above). Sharing is the norm, personal property the exception that must be arranged for. (Of course, not everything is shared with everyone. There may be adult possessions that are off-limits to children, such as ceremonial objects or family heirlooms.)

In the typical U.S. classroom, although property such as art materials and books technically belongs to the school, we behave as though children "own" their crayons or their books. If a child takes a pencil from another's desk, it may even be viewed as "stealing." In a home with a collectivistic culture, this would not be the case. A teacher may feel that a child has problems with respecting personal property, when that child has been socialized to share and expect sharing from others. A parent, told that her child has such a "problem," may be mystified. She may also begin to fear and resent having her values undermined at school.

An example of cross-cultural misunderstandings about property and sharing took place in a multicultural preschool where a Mexican-American girl came into conflict with an "Anglo" boy (Quiroz & Greenfield, 1996). The boy was playing with building blocks on the floor, and the girl began to play with some of the unused blocks near him. But the boy seemed to feel that because he had taken them off the shelf they were his to play with alone, so he hit the girl and she started to cry. The teacher scolded the girl and told her to find her own materials to play with. She later explained to the girl's mother that her daughter needed to learn to respect the rights of other children. From an individualistic point of view, the boy "owned" the blocks because he had chosen them first. From a collectivistic point of view, the blocks did not belong to anyone. They were community property. It was not even a matter of the boy's sharing the blocks. They were not his to share. An act of aggression made the boy further at fault.

Most teachers who hear this story are outraged that the teacher did not reprimand the boy for hitting. But they rarely argue with the implication that the girl should have asked the boy's permission to use the blocks. In the meantime, the teacher, the girl, and her mother were all confused. The child understood neither the behavior of her peer nor her teacher; the teacher diagnosed the child as having a problem and her mother as needing to do something about it. Not understanding the teacher's implicit values, the mother interpreted the attitude of the teacher as discriminatory toward Latinos.

RELATIONSHIP TO OTHER FRAMEWORKS
FOR UNDERSTANDING CULTURES

Other frameworks have been used in the past as ways of understanding cultural differences. We have chosen the individualism / collectivism framework because it deals with a large number of important cultural components in an integrated way. But readers may want to investigate other frameworks that complement this one. Edward Stewart (1971) developed a taxonomy that addressed the way in which cultures approach four domains: activities, social relations, the self, and the world. The orientation to "social relations" and "self" is addressed in a similar fashion within the individualism / collectivism framework. Within the "activity" domain, Stewart distinguishes among cultures that have a "being" orientation (valuing acceptance of the status quo); cultures that have a "becoming" orientation (believing that humans evolve and change); and those that have a "doing" orientation (valuing getting things done, striving to control what is happening to people). The "world" domain has to do with beliefs about humans' role and value with regard to nature and other animals and spirituality. It should come as no surprise that the dominant U.S. culture differs from the cultures of nondominant groups on all of these dimensions. A "doing" and "human-over-nature" approach typifies dominant U.S. culture.

Another framework with which readers may be familiar examines cultures with regard to the degree to which they are "high context" or "low context" (Hall, 1976). Much of the focus of this framework is on the nature of communication. In high context cultures, such as those of Japan and Mexico, a large part of the meaning of a message is implicit. It is assumed that the listener shares the values, beliefs, and norms of the speaker; so the speaker does not need to encode everything in the message itself. Speakers can get by with this because high context cultures tend to have very clear expectations about how people should behave, what roles they should take, and the meaning of various social rituals. They don't need to explain everything to each other. Low context cultures like those of the U.S., England, and Germany communicate in much more explicit language. Much less is left to shared assumptions about beliefs, values, and norms. The high-context/low-context framework describes in detail sets of behaviors that are associated with collectivistic and individualistic cultures respectively. For example, high-context cultures are associated with hierarchical, stable roles (as in collectivism) and consequent ideas of who should speak when and how; low-context cultures are associated with more egalitarian roles and consequent latitude in self-expression (as in individualism).

In other research, Hall analyzed cultures in terms of their orientations to time and space (1959, 1966). While we won't go into these analyses in depth, we will comment that people's treatment of time could also be seen as related to collectivistic and individualistic values. The cultures that tend to be less punctual tend to be the collectivistic ones (Brislin, 1993). They place greater value on attending to the needs of the person making an immediate request than on being punctual for a previously scheduled meeting. This value seems to be in line with what has been observed elsewhere about the collectivistic value of helping. Turning down a request for help is to be avoided at almost any cost in collectivistic cultures. A previously established schedule is not really responsive to human needs in many ways: It doesn't account for emergencies, weather, newly-arising problems, or people's feelings at the time.

These frameworks, along with Hofstede's treatment of individualism and collectivism (and other cultural dimensions), are well-explained in Lustig and Koester's 1999 book, *Intercultural Competence.* The challenge of understanding cultures and the role of culture in child-rearing and schooling is to find principles and frameworks that help us grasp the big picture so that we know what to pay attention to in learning about our students' lives. We believe that the individualism / collectivism framework is the most productive for our purposes because it encompasses most other frameworks and does just that: It alerts us to "big picture" issues. One reason the *Bridging Cultures* framework helps educators think more effectively about cultural influences in the classroom is that it deals with deep and broad values; these values motivate a whole array of ways of thinking and behaving.

"Multicultural education" is the umbrella term used to encompass several strands of theory and practice that have formed the basis of professional development and pre-service education for teachers (Artiles, 1996). In order to evaluate the importance and place of the *Bridging Cultures* framework, teachers and staff developers should consider where it fits within this larger picture.

STRANDS OF MULTICULTURAL EDUCATION

Curriculum Change

One strand of multicultural education has emphasized the histories and traditions of different ethnolinguistic groups and how to change instruction to reflect them. For example, to make curriculum more inclusive, teachers may develop specific lessons on African-American history or on the annexation of Mexican territory by the U.S., as part of their social studies instruction. A preferred approach to inclusion is to revise curricula and textbooks thoroughly to be more representative of the histories and traditions of groups that make up U.S. society (cf., King, 1994; Ladson-Billings, 1991). Some curricula (and the professional development related to them) characterized as "anti-racist" are directed at raising teachers' and students' awareness of how textbooks and schools' institutional practices promote unconscious racism (Derman-Sparks, Phillips, & Hilliard, 1997; Nieto, 1996; Tator & Henry, 1991). A related movement has focused on "prejudice reduction" to help students develop more democratic attitudes and behaviors (Banks, 1995).

Inclusive curricula, anti-racist curricula, and prejudice reduction education all require an understanding of how groups' histories — in particular their historical relationships to the dominant culture — shape their current realities. Groups are not on an equal playing field, and to ignore the sociopolitical histories that place them in different positions with regard to present-day U.S. society is to engage in a "naive multiculturalism" (Mesa-Bains, 1997, p. 28). Consider the different histories of an Irish-American and a Mexican-American from New Mexico. One is descended from a great-grandfather who came to the U.S. voluntarily as an immigrant in the late 1800s. The other's ancestors lived for untold generations on what became U.S. soil, but were socially displaced by the U.S. annexation of Mexican land. These two people can be expected to have very different perceptions of their relationship to the dominant U.S. culture (Mesa-Bains, 1997).

Acknowledging the racism in U.S. society, particularly institutionalized racism that perpetuates tacit beliefs and overt policies that keep people of color from educational opportunities, is absolutely essential to any meaningful reform of education. To focus on "culture" is not to deny the power of "race" in shaping the lives of students of color but to add another important dimension for understanding how to teach and design educational programs for them.

Structuring Schools for Empowerment

A second multicultural strand addresses how and to what degree schools and other social institutions promote the empowerment of all of the members of their

communities through the methods they use to involve them. The following vi-
gnette is an example of how these issues could play out in a school district.

THE PARENT ADVISORY COUNCIL

Dr. Wilson, principal of Jefferson Middle School, wants to ensure
that the parent advisory council has members from all of the ethnolinguistic groups in the district. The council is made up largely of
European-American parents at this point. She asks the council chair-
person and the PTA President to approach several parents from
other backgrounds. Three or four are successfully recruited. The
catch is that these new members are not culturally representative of
their communities. They are simply the ones who have learned to
accommodate to the dominant culture's ways of doing things. Dr.
Wilson doesn't realize that to get real participation she may have to
gradually work through community groups in ways that parents from
those groups are comfortable with. For instance, many "minority"
parents prefer to work as members of a small group and make
decisions as a group rather than individuals on a committee, each
representing a group of constituents (Delgado-Gaitan, 1990; Diaz,
2000). If this administrator had done the *Bridging Cultures* training,
she would likely have understood the parents' point of view.

Contributing to the empowerment of students from all backgrounds are
school-based practices that respond to different needs and family-based expectations while maintaining high expectations for all students (Lucas, Henze, & Donato, 1990). For example, if parents are accustomed to taking their infants and
young children with them to meetings and appointments, it may be important to
ensure that school meetings and events accommodate that practice. Such possible change would flow naturally from understanding the collectivistic perspective that generates this practice of not separating children unnecessarily from the
family.

Real parent and community empowerment depend as well on transforma-
tions in the power relations between the school (representing the dominant community) and groups that have traditionally wielded less power. One mode of empowerment is for school personnel to understand and accept a collectivistic value

perspective, although it differs from the values built into schooling. This is the path we take in this volume.

Recognizing Influences of Culture on Cognition

Another strand of multicultural education has focused on purported cognitive characteristics of members of various groups. For example, some groups have been labeled predominantly "visual" learners (e.g., John, 1972; Kleinfeld, 1970). Or, groups have been variously described as "field-dependent" or "field-independent" (Cazden & Leggett, 1981; Ramirez & Castaneda, 1974). For field-dependent people, the objects, ideas, and physical phenomena of life take on meaning only as they relate to their physical and social *context*. Field-independent people, on the other hand, often relate to objects, ideas, and physical phenomena out of context, as if they exist on their own, independent of any frame of reference. Such research often looks at individuals apart from their cultural contexts and is probably better understood when combined with a cultural perspective, such as we utilize in this volume. In cultures where the group is valued over the individual, field-dependence is a natural and desirable way of relating to the world. Likewise, when a culture values the individual over the group, it will foster field independence. Instead of being seen as an inferior mode of cognition, field interdependence (and "interdependence" is a more accurate term), in our analysis, is the cognitive manifestation of a collectivistic value system.

Translating research on cognitive differences into instructional strategies is challenging. For example, over-simplified responses, such as trying to teach mostly through the visual mode, may short-change language development necessary for school success. It is not immediately clear how these and other psychological characteristics alone would guide instructional approaches without reference to a coherent framework that puts them in context. Identifying students' strengths can lead to innovative instruction that capitalizes on such strengths, but "an over emphasis on learning styles differences may lead to a new form of inaccurate labeling and stereotyping…, or, even worse, diagnoses of brain differences or genetic differences" (More, 1989, p. 25). Without understanding why children in subsistence cultures (such as some Alaska Natives) might need to have highly-developed visual skills, a teacher might draw false conclusions about those children's capacity to learn other kinds of skills. Our notions of creating a bridge between home culture and school culture might be a useful metaphor for dealing with differences in learning style. For example, visual skills can and should be utilized in the classroom. Indeed, they are critical in modern computer technology

(Greenfield & Cocking, 1994), but visual materials and skills can also be utilized as a bridge to the development of verbal skills.

Understanding Culture's Influence on the Social Processes of Teaching and Learning

A fourth strand in multicultural education has drawn from sociolinguistics and anthropology to examine relationship and communication patterns within certain groups and develop parallel classroom processes that foster student participation (Au, 1980; Heath, 1983; Michaels, 1981). For example, researchers worked with educators on the Navajo reservation to develop a portfolio assessment process that was culturally harmonious (Koelsch & Estrin, 1996). In many traditional American Indian communities,[2] children are typically assessed through observation as they engage in a meaningful activity — not through isolated tasks administered at arbitrary times or through verbal questioning. Portfolio assessment is appealing because it does not require students to be tested outside of a meaningful context; rather, the products of daily instruction can be evaluated against sets of criteria to determine how well students are doing. The emphasis on cultural values in our *Bridging Cultures* framework leads us to understand *why* a meaningful context might be important to American Indian children. Within the collectivistic perspective, cognitive skills are not valued for their own sake but only insofar as they contribute to a socially useful function. A meaningful context often provides such a function.

CONCLUSION

Cochran-Smith has said, "What we need in the teaching profession are not better generic strategies for 'doing multicultural education' or 'teaching for diversity' nor more lesson plans about basket making, piñatas, and other customs in non-Anglo cultures. There are no particular lessons or units teacher can include in their classrooms that will make them 'culturally responsive' or 'inclusive' teachers. By the same token, in the context of professional development, there is no particular activity a staff developer can use to turn 'culturally unresponsive' or 'monocultural' teachers into responsive and multicultural ones" (1997, p. 29). By providing

---

[2] There are significant differences among American Indian communities, and one cannot make assumptions about one on the basis of knowledge of another. However, accounts from many Indian groups suggest that the kinds of communication and assessment strategies used in most U.S. schools are culturally incompatible with those that prevail in their own homes and communities.

a framework that helps teachers understand their own underlying cultural value system and how this may differ from that of their students and their students' parents, *Bridging Cultures* responds to the gap Cochran-Smith identifies. The framework enables teachers to become culturally responsive and culturally inclusive. When teachers become aware of cultural values and cultural differences at a deep level they can use any of the other tools (expanding curriculum, e.g.) in a more powerful and culturally appropriate manner.

With any of the areas of potential conflict between different value orientations, the key to problem-solving is awareness. Recognizing the possible barriers to cross-cultural understanding leads to different interpretations of situations, or at least the realization that there is more than one possible interpretation. When both teachers and parents are aware of their somewhat different orientations, they have a greater chance of forging alliances and discovering *shared goals* for children. Communication between parents and teachers can become more comfortable and productive for all concerned. Children, too, can become more aware of the differences between home and school cultures, more conscious of the kinds of choices they are making. In addition, they may learn to talk about different approaches to solving the same problem and the pros and cons of each.

In conclusion, we argue that the *Bridging Cultures* framework is a necessary foundation for the most effective utilization of other multicultural approaches. It enables teachers and school personnel to understand why other approaches may (or may not) work with diverse populations. It also provides a tool for evaluating the cultural compatibility of these approaches for the many groups who come to school carrying a collectivistic value system with them.

Questions for Reflection and Research

1. How would you respond to "The Jobs Scenario"? Did you respond more in favor of finding a third person (and thus protecting the individual assignment of the task) or helping (supporting the interdependence of classmates)?
2. Think about the values and beliefs that guided your family of origin. Looking at Table 1.1, consider which kinds of values were emphasized most in your family. How are these values reflected in your teaching practices?
3. Make a chart with the elements from Table 1.1. Write down examples from your classroom experience that illustrate individualism or collectivism operating. Which cultural values are dominant?
4. What do you find most powerful about the framework of individualism and collectivism?
5. What do you see as limitations to the framework?

Further Reading

Greenfield, P.M. & Cocking, R. R. (Eds.), (1994). *Cross-cultural roots of minority child development.* Hillsdale, NJ: Lawrence Erlbaum Associates.

Hollins, E. R. (1996). *Culture in school learning.* Mahwah, NJ: Lawrence Erlbaum Associates.

Lustig, M. W. & Koester, J. (1999). *Intercultural competence: Interpersonal communication across cultures* (Third Edition). New York: Longman.

Rothstein-Fisch, C., Greenfield, P.M. & Trumbull, E. (1999). *Bridging cultures* with classroom strategies. *Educational Leadership*, 56(7), 64-67.

Valdés, G. (1996). *Con Respeto.* New York: Teachers College Press.

chapter 2

Parent Involvement: Recommended but Not Always Successful

In this chapter we review traditional approaches to parent involvement and examine some of their limitations when applied to non-dominant communities. We do this not to disparage efforts that may prove successful for some families and schools, but to point to ways to expand that success to others. We hope our critique, elaborated in many examples, will help schools and teachers understand the issues and develop strategies for reaching a larger range of parents.

The mountain of research showing that parent involvement contributes significantly to student achievement and other positive outcomes[1] has resulted in a near-universal mandate across public school districts to find new ways to engage parents in their children's school experience. A national survey showed that during the 1995-96 school year, 92% of public elementary schools held some kind of activities intended to encourage parent involvement (Carey, Lewis, & Farris, 1998). In fact, eligibility for certain federal funding depends on districts' establishing parent advisory councils and/or engaging parents in other activities to promote parent and family involvement in schools. Specifically, Title I of the Elementary and Secondary Education Act, amended by the Improving America's Schools

---

[1] See Chavkin, 1993; Comer & Haynes, 1991; Davies, 1991; Epstein, 1989, 1991, 1993, 1994; Henderson & Berla, 1994; Hoover-Dempsey & Sandler, 1997; National Education Goals Panel, 1995; Rutherford, 1995; U.S. Department of Education, 1994.

Act of 1994, provides funds for schools to offer opportunities for at-risk children and their families. Every school receiving Title I funds must develop a compact that clarifies what schools and families can do to support children's learning. In addition, Goal 8 of the U.S. National Education Goals states that by the year 2000, "Every school will promote partnerships that will increase parental involvement and participation in promoting the social, emotional, and academic growth of children" (H.R. 1804, Sec. 102 (8), 1994).

In 1997, through the Partnership for Family Involvement in Education, the U.S. Department of Education published *A Compact for Learning: An Action Handbook for Family-School Partnerships* (De Kanter, Ginsburg, Pederson, Peterson, & Rich, 1997). It suggests a format for writing a compact between families and schools based on intensified academic standards and high expectations of achievement. Central to this task is "shared responsibility for effective, frequent communication between school and home" (p. 11). According to the *Handbook*, developing a five-step compact includes: (1) coming together as a team, (2) creating a compact, (3) using the compact, (4) evaluating the compact, and (5) strengthening the compact. The compact appears to be a worthwhile endeavor, where school and home values are consonant with one another. However, this is not always the case.

Indeed, only two compacts cited acknowledge the role of language or culture. The compact of Hueco Elementary School in El Paso, Texas, noted that, "Families of Hispanic students are not involved at the school because of a language barrier" (De Kanter, et al., 1997, p. 33). The perceived problem resulted in providing all family-school communications in Spanish and English. Unfortunately, this strategy does not directly address the underlying cultural issues. It is a common response in such settings to focus on language rather than on communication problems caused by cultural differences.

A more potent intervention occurred in Stockton, California. When teachers and school staff were unsure how to work with diverse families they established a "mentor parent" program. Mentor parents conducted workshops on involvement in school, overcoming parents' negative school experiences and addressing teacher bias resulting from "cultural or language differences between teacher and parent" (De Kanter, et al., 1997, p. 33). Stockton is an extremely diverse community, which has experienced an influx of Cambodian, Vietnamese, and Hmong (a tribal people from Laos) immigrants in the last ten or more years to complement an existing population that was already somewhat diverse. These examples can be kept in mind as the two sections below are read.

The underlying assumption of common goals among parents of various backgrounds and their children's schools may be faulty. In fact, "the literature reveals that the perceptions of parents and school personnel concerning the purposes, goals, and outcomes of schooling may differ dramatically" (Rutherford, 1995, p. 21). Blame over failure to achieve these presumed "common" goals is often assigned to both parents and schools, when in fact the real problem is they don't have *commonly defined* goals. Although cultural differences may be cited as a reason, it seems to us that it is rare that schools (or those in charge of them) get below the surface to understand how those differences can lead not only to different goals but also completely different views of schooling and, hence, parent involvement.

Cross-cultural research suggests that there is no universally successful way to involve parents.[2] Even what people consider "involvement" is culturally variable. Parents may fear that certain kinds of involvement taken for granted in U.S. schools — e.g., questioning teachers about assignments or grades — will be interpreted as interference or disrespect. In particular, the roles that parents or teachers take on differ markedly across cultures. The concept of a parent's teaching academic skills at home may be an alien one. The fact is that because of conflicting values at home and school (see Chapter 1), many immigrant parents do not welcome parenting advice. Moreover, large segments of immigrant communities (e.g., from Mexico) have had little opportunity for formal education in their homelands and may therefore not be prepared to help their children with school work or to volunteer in any academic capacity in their children's classrooms (Finders & Lewis, 1994). Having homework in Spanish, of course, may sometimes facilitate immigrant Latino parents' participation in helping with assignments (Diaz, 1999), but knowing the level of parents' formal education is at least as important. We need to be somewhat wary of global recommendations for parent "leadership," as well. Leadership does not take the same form across cultures. Therefore, to evaluate "best practices" in parent involvement, we must examine how culture influences parent participation as well as schools' approaches to parents.[3]

After a short review of issues in cross-cultural parent involvement, this chapter examines the standard wisdom on how parents should be involved in their

---

[2] See Allexsaht-Snider, 1992; Cochran & Dean, 1991; Delgado-Gaitan, 1992; Goldenberg & Gallimore, 1995; Gorman & Balter, 1997; Greenfield, Quiroz, & Raeff, 2000; Greenfield, Raeff, & Quiroz, 1996; Hoover-Dempsey & Sandler, 1997; Simich-Dudgeon, 1993.

[3] For examples of guidelines for parent involvement, see Center on Organization and Restructuring of Schools, 1994; Epstein, 1993; Moles, 1996; Morris, Taylor, Knight , & Wasson, 1995; Oregon State Department of Education, 1990; the documents of the Center on School, Family, and Community Partnerships at Johns Hopkins University; and the Web site, H.R. 1804 Goals 2000: Educate America Act (http://www.ed.gov/legislation/GOALS2000/TheAct/sec102.html).

children's schooling and critiques it from a cultural perspective. As the reader may expect, we assess the "best practices" in terms of how well they seem to work for parents and families from nondominant cultures — in particular, from collectivistic cultures. The chapter concludes with recommendations for improving parent programs so that they are more responsive to parents who do not share the individualistic orientation of the dominant culture.

"MINORITY" PARENT INVOLVEMENT

Research suggests that while parent involvement has increased over the last two decades, "minority" (the term usually used in the educational literature) parents and those from lower socioeconomic groups have had a "lower level of contact with schools than their better-off counterparts" (Moles, 1993, p. 28). Parents who are less involved and visible in the school are often assumed to be less interested in their children's education (Casanova, 1996). The lack of contact, however, is not for lack of interest. According to a survey of 2,000 parents conducted by Metropolitan Life in 1987, inner-city parents were less satisfied than suburban parents with the amount of contact they were getting with teachers. They wanted more.

Studies of immigrant Latino families have repeatedly shown that parents are highly interested in being involved in their children's education (see Allexsaht-Snider, 1992; Diaz, 2000; Delgado-Gaitan, 1992; Goldenberg & Gallimore, 1995). It should be noted that it is most often the mothers who do get involved, and it is they (as compared to fathers) who are most likely to have the role of looking out for their children's education (Diaz, 2000; Klimes-Dougan, Lopez, Nelson, & Adelman, 1992). However, as we show, the same cross-cultural value conflict described in Chapter 1 leads Latino immigrant parents from Mexico and Central America to desire one kind of involvement, while school personnel have strong preferences for another. Other studies including African-American parents have reported the same finding: high interest without the necessary conditions to support involvement (see, e.g., Chavkin & Williams, 1993). Nevertheless, social and cultural differences between home and school are rarely investigated as a reason for lower involvement, unless they are invoked as a source of deficiency in parenting (Casanova, 1996).

Something that must be mentioned in this context is that traditional approaches to "minority" parent involvement often fail to acknowledge how the distribution of power, resources, and knowledge prevents meaningful engagement of many sectors of the wider community in schooling (Young, 1999). In fact, the social inequalities seen in the broader society tend to be maintained in relations between members of the dominant culture (including school personnel) and members of other cultures (Fine, 1993). Schools may actually "facilitate the exclusion of students and parents by (consciously or unconsciously) establishing activities that require specific majority culturally based knowledge and behaviors about the school as an institution. Frequently, these ideas are assumed and are not made explicit" (Delgado-Gaitan, 1991, p. 21).

PARENT-SCHOOL PARTNERSHIPS:
RESPONSIBILITIES OF PARENTS AND SCHOOLS

Joyce Epstein's work over nearly two decades has been the benchmark educators look to for understanding how to work with parents — and more recently with the wider community. From student reactions to the ways teachers attempt to involve parents (Epstein & Becker, 1982) to school and family partnerships (Epstein, 1998b), she has provided the field with theory and practice on how to link home, school, and community. Our goal is to expand on this groundwork by elucidating the cross-cultural issues in home-school relationships and how they may unconsciously inhibit parent involvement.

As Director of the National Network of Partnership Schools, Epstein believes "the expertise — knowledge, actions, and will — of educators, families, communities, students, and researchers all are essential for developing, implementing, evaluating, and continually improving programs of school, family and community partnerships" (1998b, p. 2). As of February 1999, the National Network of Partnership Schools included 932 schools and 115 districts among its membership. The Network's Web site (www.csos.jhu.edu/p2000) contains a wide range of publications, information about membership and services, and links to specific partner programs. We believe it worthwhile to highlight potential opportunities for partnerships to improve their responsiveness to families from different cultural backgrounds.

Because Epstein has earned a reputation for leadership in drawing attention to and researching relationships between home and school, her work becomes the starting point for our discussion of parent-school partnerships and parent involvement. The *Handbook of Parenting* (Connors & Epstein, 1995) identifies six areas of responsibility of schools and parents in partnerships. These include parenting; communicating: volunteering; home enrichment; decision making, governance and advocacy; and collaboration with community.

These responsibilities may fall primarily on parents, primarily on schools, or on both. For example, even though "Parenting" (below) is of course largely a parental responsibility, schools are now expected to provide parenting education courses (see the provisions of Goals 2000: Educate America Act, cited at http://

www.ed.gov/pubs/G2KReforming/app_c.html). Each of these responsibilities will be described and followed by a discussion of how the general goals for parents may — or may not — relate to the needs of families from nondominant cultures, specifically families operating from a more collectivistic value framework than that of the dominant culture.

1. Basic Obligations of Families — Parenting

According to the *Handbook,* "Schools provide information to families about children's health and safety, supervision, nutrition, discipline and guidance, and other parenting skills and child-rearing approaches… Schools are enriched and educators and youngsters are enlightened when families share their background, cultures, skills and interests in class or school programs and activities" (Connors & Epstein, 1995, p. 447). However, different cultural value orientations lead to different and equally valid beliefs about guidance, parenting skills, and child-rearing approaches (Greenfield, 1994). The goals (e.g., interdependence versus independence) and direction (e.g., helping others versus taking care of one's own needs) of child development depend upon the family's cultural value system. Schools should not assume that they hold the ultimate understanding of child and adolescent development. In fact, parents may have one developmental script for their children and the schools a very different one (Greenfield, 1994).

The issue of "parenting" vis-à-vis parent-school partnerships may be more complex than a simple exchange of information can accommodate. As we found, the values and child-rearing practices of immigrant parents from Mexico and Central America may conflict with school values and expectations. Consider Valdés' description of the immigrant Mexican families with whom she worked:

> For all of their virtues, however, for all of their dedication to raising good human beings and responsible adults, in the eyes of their teachers, the parents were failing their children. They did not respond to school communications in a timely fashion. They did not help their children at home. And they seemed not to have understood that without education their children would never be able to "make something of oneself." In fact, they worried little about individual achievement in mainstream terms. They were guided by beliefs about child rearing that emphasized respect and obedience. They did not understand the mother's role to include teaching school lessons to her children (Valdés, 1996, p. 201).

Parenting Education

Schools have often concluded that parents need instruction in how to parent their children. For this reason, a great many parent education programs have been developed that generally focus on imparting information. Topics may include discipline, health, or how to promote student learning. Many parent education programs are merely Spanish translations of traditional programs (Gorman & Balter, 1997). Yet the goals of discipline, health education, or student learning may be quite different in different cultures; and the means to achieving them may not translate readily across cultures, particularly when one culture is individualistic and the other is collectivistic. Virtually all parents have a strong sense of how to rear their children. But rather than building on parents' strengths, programs may treat parents as if they do not know how to rear children. "…[S]chools often tell parents what they must do. This results in a negative perception that the school is demanding and not family-friendly" (Onikama, Hammond, & Koki, 1998, p. 12). Such a strategy can lower parents' confidence in their own parenting competence and/or make them resent the schools for undermining the more socially oriented developmental goals, such as learning how to care for a younger sibling. Recall (from Chapter 1, the "Jobs Scenario") the discrepant attitudes between Latino immigrant parents in Los Angeles and their children's teachers about the importance of socializing children to be helpful.

2. Basic Obligations of Schools — Communicating

Schools send a variety of communications to parents: notes, newsletters, report cards, and meeting announcements. Parents may also receive phone calls from teachers asking about a student or sharing information about school. In most cases, however, students are the conduits of messages between school and home. Despite schools' best intentions, these communications may pose difficulty for parents who must negotiate a different language, a different set of communication styles, and a different orientation to child development. For example, many parents may misunderstand the complicated conditions in California for obtaining bilingual education for their children. One wonders whether communication is at times intentionally ambiguous or convoluted — actually designed to *prevent* parents from knowing how to respond and express their desires. Sometimes what schools claim to be promoting and what actually appears to happen are at odds with each other (Young, 1999).

Potential Miscommunication

Valdés (1996) cites a powerful instance of miscommunication from her ethnographic research with immigrant Latino families. An eight-year-old child was given the responsibility of verbally conveying a message to his brother's teacher: His younger brother was allergic to fish and was not to be given fish at lunch time. It is unclear whether the message was not actually conveyed, or the teacher did not believe it was her role to pass it on to the correct authorities. In any case, the child continued to be given fish along with the other children and, as a result, missed school for several days after each fish lunch. The unfortunate outcome was that the mother came to perceive that the school did not really care about her son.

Valdés comments, "Had Velma (the mother) sent a note instead of a message, it might have been that she would have received some response from the teacher or another individual. Velma, however, did not know that in American schools, the appropriate way of handling such matters involves either talking to the teacher personally or sending a note. Velma had no way of knowing that sending an oral message via a slightly older child might not be taken seriously" (1996, p. 156). Yet in Mexico, children are trained and expected to be a dependable means of communication between adults; apparently, the teacher was unaware of this cultural strength of immigrant Mexican families (Valdés, 1996).

In the situation described above, Valdés's research assistant tried to convey the idea that written notes are most effective in communicating health and other concerns to school officials. However, because of this incident and others, the mother was too outraged to focus on the note-writing suggestion. Instead, she felt that the school was unresponsive and believed her only recourse would be to remove her child from the school. Parents may find notes too impersonal — whether from school to home or vice versa. They may believe that face to face communication is more cordial and appropriate, especially when the topic is serious or sensitive. Moreover, parents' limited literacy skills may make oral communication an absolute necessity. In this case, "normal" school customs concerning communication were an invitation for cross-cultural miscommunication.

Parents' Perceptions of School Communications

When schools send notices home about services they are offering or opportunities for parents to participate in an activity, they may not give consideration to the form these notices take. Teachers in an urban California district with high numbers of Chinese, Latino, African-American, and Vietnamese immigrants reported the following: "Written forms go home for one service or another, forms that are often hard to read, invasive, or potentially insulting — a 'communication' strategy that seems designed to increase the distance between home and school" (Dyson, et al., 1997, p. 38). The parent may be required to complete these forms in order for a child to receive Title 1 program support or speech therapy, for example. Some parents or guardians don't like filling out forms that ask for a huge amount of personal information because they question whether confidentiality can be assured or they don't know the answers to certain questions. So, as a result, children may go without services to which they are entitled, such as free lunch; and school officials may draw unwarranted conclusions about parents' degree of concern for their own children's welfare.

McCaleb (1997) did a study with parents of first-graders in a Spanish immersion program in San Francisco that had about 43% Spanish-language dominant and 37% African-American students. Parents were interviewed about their involvement with their children's school. Responses of some of these parents reveal the dangers of generalizing about why parents aren't involved in the ways schools expect. One parent commented, "I think that there hasn't been enough communication from the school to the homes. We only receive notices to come to meetings. I feel that we all need the administration to establish more contact with families and invite parents to participate more" (McCaleb, 1997, p. 93). Perhaps in this parent's eyes, opportunities to communicate in ways other than formal meetings would be desirable. Or she might be more responsive to a direct invitation, not an impersonal announcement. Indeed, a hallmark of the collectivistic value system described in Chapter 1 is the centrality of personal communication and relationships with family and other intimates. Communication from unknown people in an impersonal manner is foreign to this type of culture.

Another parent in the same study, when asked about communication with the teachers, said, "When I have expressed my opinions, they have helped me, but in reality there is no partnership. I follow what the school tells me to do [with my child], what the school asks of me. It's as if I were also a student in the school" (McCaleb, 1997, p. 94). The parent seems to feel that she is in an inferior position, that the expectation is for her to comply with what the school thinks is best. Not only parents whose home language is Spanish, but also African-American parents, complain of communication difficulties with schools, demonstrating that the problem is not just "language," as is often assumed (McCaleb, 1997, p. 94). Our research indicates that parents want school personnel to respect the social values they are trying to inculcate in their children, even when they differ from the school's implicit value system. Communication problems arise when schools do not provide culturally appropriate ways to share and elicit important information about children.

Parent Involvement in Academics

A more recent trend in school-parent relations is the effort to bring parents *into* the school with the express purpose of fostering children's academic success (see "3. Volunteering," below). Parent involvement programs aim to attract classroom volunteers, encourage parent participation at school functions, and promote tutoring skills (see "4. Involvement in Learning Activities," below). This last thrust is very similar in orientation to the more general parent education programs described above, except that the exclusive focus of involvement is academic. But how will parents with a collectivistic value perspective feel about programs that emphasize academics to the exclusion of social development?

3. Involvement in Schools — Volunteering

Connors and Epstein recommend that "families can take the initiative to find ways to contribute time or talent to their children's school" (1995, p. 448). However, it would be very difficult for a parent unfamiliar with U.S. schools to "take the initiative" when the school environment includes an unfamiliar language, different norms of communication, and a seemingly curious assortment of teaching and learning methods. In the community Valdés studied, immigrant parents were embarrassed and "found almost any excuse not to go to the school and *'ponerse en evidencia'* (show how ignorant or incapable they were). Even when some parents were deeply committed to their children doing well in school... they hesitated to speak to the teacher herself" (Valdés, 1996, p. 162).

Volunteering also takes time, a precious commodity for low-income families, whose wage earners may work more than one job. Nevertheless, some research suggests that women who work outside the home are the most likely to become involved in their children's schools (Delgado-Gaitan & Segura, 1989; Diaz, 2000). Several of the parents in McCaleb's study blamed themselves for their less-than-successful attempts to be included in their children's school. One said, "The only problem is that parents don't have time, or we don't make time for this. I think that in this area we are failing as parents. It is important to have more interest in helping the teacher..." (McCaleb, 1997, p. 91). If volunteering is a goal, how can programs accommodate the varying schedules, cultural values, and educational levels of parents? Chapter 4 offers suggestions made by one *Bridging Cultures* teacher, who was able to increase the number of volunteers in her classroom from one to twelve.

4. Involvement in Learning Activities at Home

Connors and Epstein (1995) suggest an array of methods whereby parents can become involved with their children's schoolwork at home. For example, they suggest helping "families to become more knowledgeable partners about the school curricula and teachers' instructional methods; the academic and other skills required to pass each grade; the work their children are doing in class; how to support, monitor, discuss and help with homework; and how to help students practice and study for tests" (Connors & Epstein, 1995, p. 448). Yet, according to Valdés, "When American teachers expected that Mexican working-class mothers would 'help' their children with their schoolwork, they were making assumptions about abilities that the mothers did not have. Moreover, they were also making assumptions about the universality of what, in American schools, counts as knowledge" (1996, p. 166). Concerning academic skills, it is important to realize that for most poor people in Mexico only elementary education is available.

There are two issues here, both of which we have alluded to. First, parents limited in formal literacy skills (in English or Spanish) or with little experience in schools cannot be assumed to be helping children with schoolwork in the way teachers expect. This is particularly true when those expectations are implicit or entail new routines for parents themselves. Second, parents may not believe it is necessarily their role to help with academics because that is the domain of the professional teacher. Their role focuses on raising respectful, well-behaved human beings. Nevertheless, such a difference in values and skills does not mean that educators should give up on finding ways to involve parents.

A more likely scenario than parents' engaging directly in tutoring or helping with homework is one in which older siblings help younger ones. This is culturally harmonious (enacting the value of familial helpfulness), and it solves the problem of limited parental education. In some cases, schools have been able to persuade parents to take on an academic role with their children. Studying the literacy development of immigrant Latino children, Goldenberg and Gallimore (1995) found that worksheets on phonics that were designed in traditional ways seemed to make more sense to parents and thus could engage parents more in helping their children. "In short, the congruence between the worksheets and the parents' beliefs led to their effective use in the home, and the more children used the worksheets at home, the higher their literacy attainment at the end of the school year" (Goldenberg & Gallimore, 1995, p. 219). So, for those parents who show an interest in taking an academic role (perhaps those who have been in the United States for some time and had other children go through the school system), it would be important to identify the kinds of activities with which they are comfortable.

To help promote more learning activities at home, Epstein has developed the TIPS program: Teachers Involve Parents in Schoolwork. The function of the program is to "help families keep track of what their children are learning in school, how their children are completing their work, and whether their children are making progress or meeting problems in learning. To ensure that all families monitor their children's homework, teachers may design some homework that requires students to *talk with someone at home* about something interesting they are learning in class" (Epstein, 1998a, pp. 2-3). How this applies to families with limited formal education and limited English proficiency presents a problem: How will adults in a traditional collectivistic home, where information is supposed to flow from elder to younger, react to the child's providing information about what he or she has learned?

A promising approach is taken by the Child Development Project, which developed a literature-based moral development program that teaches children about caring, community, and personal responsibility (a mix of individualistic and collectivistic values). It uses "family homework" activities that draw on family experiences to connect home and school (Developmental Studies Center, 1995). Fourth-graders may be given the assignment of interviewing a grandparent or other elder to find out what life was like when he or she was young. The assignment not only emphasizes respect for the knowledge of elders, but it can also result in classroom discussions that highlight other values of the family. Teachers of older children (fourth grade and above) routinely ask students how an activity might be modified to make it work for them — an acknowledgment that not just any activity works for any student's family.

5. Involvement in Decision Making, Governance, and Advocacy

Connors and Epstein suggest that participation in school-based organizations (Parent-Teacher Association, Parent-Teacher Organization, Parent-Teacher-Student Association) strengthens parent involvement in children's schooling. "A parent organization may take leadership in organizing ideas that need to be discussed to improve classroom programs or practices" (Connors & Epstein, 1995, p. 449). This may be an unrealistic expectation. It is unlikely that parents intimidated by the school would take an advocacy position. Also, the collectivistic system — based on an agricultural model of small, stable, kin-based groups — makes secondary organizations of strangers, such as the PTA, very unfamiliar as a mode of social life. However, this does not mean that parents are passive. In one case (described in Chapter 1), when a school tried to stop families from having breakfast with their children by locking them out of the schoolyard, there was a major blow-up. Latino immigrant parents who had previously not been involved in school affairs suddenly became activists. Contrary to the school officials' beliefs, parents were not trying to "steal" the food of their children. Rather, they viewed eating together as a natural part of family life. The blow-up occurred because parents' values were misunderstood and challenged (Greenfield, Raeff, & Quiroz, 1996).

It is not surprising that true parent activism, involving decision-making, may be more likely when parents are able to work together in a collective (Diaz, 2000). In such a way, they can develop skills together (see discussion of COPLA, following, as an example). Once some Latino parents join, others are more likely to do so.

Parent Empowerment

The concept of "empowerment," evoking images of overcoming social inequity, racism, and exploitation, is associated with Brazilian educational reformer Paulo Freire (1970). At best, parent empowerment programs try to demystify American education and promote parental influence on the power structure of schools. "At worst, such empowerment programs are warmed-over parent education programs in which families are persuaded that if they change their behavior at home, all will be well, in school and in the world, with their children" (Valdés, 1996, p. 195). Parent empowerment programs can be successful, or they can result in abysmal failure and frustration, depending in part on the level of mutuality between parents and school.

One successful program is COPLA (*Comite de Padres Latinos*), organized by researcher Concha Delgado-Gaitan in collaboration with Spanish-speaking immigrant parents of preschool-age children to share strategies for adjusting to their new community and schools. COPLA stresses maintaining Spanish-language and Mexican cultural values along with getting a cooperative dialogue going with the schools. One of the primary goals of these parents is to see that the schools provide effective bilingual programs for their children (Delgado-Gaitan, 1994). Immigrant families involved with COPLA wanted to instill their own values (e.g., respect and cooperation) and still ensure that their children were able to participate in U.S. society successfully. They learned how to expand their range of language patterns to include those used in school. COPLA is one model for empowerment that seems to merge collectivistic values and behaviors with the schools' individualistic orientation. In this case, interdependence and helpfulness, two prominent collectivistic values, helped to create and sustain an active advocacy group. Within that group, parents learned how their involvement could help their children and have an impact on educational practices.

It should be acknowledged that advocacy can come with some risks. Schools may not realize that parents' ways of participating can conflict with schools' expectations. Educational researcher Julie Aronson (1996) cites an example from Hawaii, a state with great cultural and linguistic diversity. When parents became very involved in administrative, curricular, and instructional decisions, the administration and teachers reacted defensively. As a result, parents' advocacy was thwarted, and parents felt betrayed.

6. Collaboration and Exchanges with the Community

According to Connors and Epstein, community involvement "includes schools' efforts to inform students and families about community and support services or provide or coordinate access to services such as after-school recreation, tutorial programs, health services, cultural events, and other programs" (1995, p. 449). Linking community services directly to the school site can be done through parent resource centers.

Parent resource centers can support parents as they learn about schools and seek to help their children. In addition, they create a safe, trusted environment where guidance is available on how to get information on educational opportunities and health and social services (Moles, 1996). As families become more acquainted with the mainstream culture via familiar and friendly schools, they can better utilize the resources of the broader community. The greatest virtue of the parent resource center is that it allows a consolidated effort to develop among the community, school, and families to promote student success.

Title IV of the Goals 2000: Educate America Act provides funding for "Parent Information and Resource Centers" that operate at state or regional level. These are intended to help strengthen partnerships between school and social service professionals and families so that families can learn more about child-rearing and schooling. These are distinct from locally organized parent resource centers but reflect the degree to which the expectation for parent involvement in school has been institutionalized. In 1998, the federal government gave $25,000,000 to states to fund such centers.

In our experience, parent resource centers, or better yet, "family resource centers,"[4] work best when they have a home-like atmosphere. If parent resource

---

[4] The term "family resource center" is more appropriate because it acknowledges the importance of extended family to many who would use it. We use "parent resource center" because of its links to literature and legislation on parent involvement.

centers are to be maximally successful, they should be centrally located in the school, conveying the message that families are valued partners in education. Ideally, centers should be equipped with kitchens and bathrooms, soft furniture, resource information in many languages, telephone and computer access, and toys for small children. When the center welcomes the whole family — including children of all ages — parents or grandparents can access the resources available to them more easily. Even more important, making the whole family welcome displays the school's respect for the family as a unit. This is crucial to families with a collectivistic value orientation, who may feel that the school is driving a wedge into the family as a unified group by treating each child as an individual. Center personnel should be drawn from the parent population itself. Thus, parents, knowledgeable about the language and customs of both home and school, can provide the information necessary to best help other parents find resources in the community. Often this information derives from the personal experiences of these parents, who have had children in the school system for several years and have learned to how to interact successfully with the school. Parents who choose to participate in this way are likely to have leadership roles in their communities as well.

This discussion of the expectations schools hold for parents and some of the difficulties encountered by both sides gives us a healthy respect for the role of culture in child-rearing and schooling, as well as for the challenges of developing true cross-cultural understanding. In the remaining sections of the chapter we probe some of the key factors in cross-cultural parent involvement in greater depth and point to positive steps schools can take to find common ground with parents.

FACTORS INFLUENCING PARENT PARTICIPATION

Role Expectations

To understand why parents become involved in their children's education, researchers have investigated how parents view their own role. This "role construction" incorporates beliefs about the parenting role, about child development, and about "appropriate parental home-support roles in children's education" (Hoover-Dempsey & Sandler, 1997, p. 9). Parents' ideas about their role are intertwined with the vision they have of "the ideal child." This vision guides their parenting practices and how they interpret their children's behaviors. Some parents place a high value on conformity, obedience, and good behavior (a collectivistic orientation characteristic of immigrant Latino parents from Mexico and Central America). Such parents usually see their role as raising respectful children with a strong work ethic who are obedient to proper authority. Others value self-respect and self-reliance more highly, reflecting an individualistic orientation that is characteristic of European-American parents and schools. Those embracing the latter values also tend to believe they should take on the roles of academic tutor, guide, and outspoken advocate expected by schools. Because of such different notions of parental role, collectivistic parents can quickly find themselves in a conflicting relationship with their children's schools.

In reality, culture is often almost completely overlooked in explanations of why parents do not become involved in the ways schools expect. For example, educators may assume that a parent resists taking on the role of academic coach because she lacks a sense of competence (hence the myriad forms of instruction for parents, including letters to home, injunctions at parent conference time, and actual courses). However, immigrant parents from Mexico and Central America are not likely to consider it appropriate for them to teach their children in these ways. The groups parents belong to exert a strong socializing influence on parents' role construction, therefore it is necessary to understand the individual's parental role as embedded within a particular culture or set of cultures.

As already discussed, immigrant parents from Mexico and Central America may see themselves primarily as socializing agents (Greenfield, Quiroz, & Raeff, 2000). According to that vision, the role of parents is to "talk with or counsel their children concerning correct and incorrect behavior" (Goldenberg & Gallimore, 1995, p. 201). The belief is that only by being a good person with proper behavior can one develop cognitively and succeed academically. In fact, in Mexican culture, to be well-educated ("*bien educado*," in Spanish) is to be well-mannered, kind, and respectful (Delgado-Gaitan, 1992). Similarly, Vietnamese-American parents strive to rear their children to be "well-rounded persons who will be knowledge-able and well-mannered...In their view, education should also provide moral guidance" (California Department of Education, 1994, p. 22). Despite their belief in the importance of education, Vietnamese-American parents' attitudes toward parent involvement may seem passive to teachers and administrators. "Very few Vietnam-ese parents join parents' advisory committees, and even fewer participate in activities programs in schools. They are often reluctant to voice their concerns and discuss educational issues with teachers and administrators" (California Depart-ment of Education, 1994, pp. 22-23). One reason is their perception that the primary responsibility for education rests with teachers and administrators.

Parents sometimes hold expectations of teachers that differ from those of the dominant culture. In some cases, immigrant parents face family crises, and, without the familiar support system of the extended family, they may seek counsel-ing advice from teachers. For example, teachers report that mothers often use conference time to discuss family-based problems such as domestic violence or alcoholism. Indeed, teachers report a variety of other types of "crisis intervention" roles. In Oakland, California one teacher found herself in an unexpected role. The mother of one of her Vietnamese students came to school one day and asked her to tell her son that he should not play video games every night. "You tell him to only play video games on Friday," she requested. Then she asked her to "tell him to eat his soup." So, the teacher talked with her student about these issues, and the mother reported later that things had improved (Dyson et al., 1997, pp. 52-53). *Bridging Cultures* teachers report similar requests from parents. Says Mrs. Hernandez, "Parents have continuously sought my advice on parenting and academic situations. Recently a parent whose child I had [in my classroom] asked what she should do with a stepchild that she caught doing something seriously wrong. She said she thought I might be able to help her discipline the child, since I work with so many kids." Note that a parent may ask for advice or intervention in the context of a personal relationship with the teacher. The same parent may perceive formal parenting classes as presumptuous on the part of the school.

Sense of Efficacy

Another factor researchers have considered for an explanation of why parents become involved (or not) in their children's education is parents' sense of *their own efficacy*. Self-efficacy, in this context, is defined as "the extent to which parents believe that through their involvement they can exert positive influence on their children's educational outcomes" (Hoover-Dempsey & Sandler, 1997, p. 3). But this concept does not take account of the fact that parents from collectivistic backgrounds may simply respect the authority of the teacher.

Immigrant parents of school-age children may feel social pressure to conform to a set of cultural norms that qualifies one as a member of the school culture. Not to know these norms is to be regarded as "immature, ignorant, stupid, incompetent, or unfit…as a parent" (Goodnow & Collins, 1990, p. 85). Without cultural knowledge of U.S. schools or a command of English, parents may actually be correct in feeling incompetent to interact in the expected ways. Nevertheless, it is unwise to assume that incompetence or lack of self-efficacy alone accounts for parents' reluctance to participate in certain ways.

Invitations from School

A third determining factor in parents' decisions to become involved in their children's schooling is the nature of the invitations they receive from schools (Hoover-Dempsey & Sandler, 1997). Given the right invitations, parents can and will become partners with teachers. Teachers reach out to parents in a variety of ways, and it matters how they do so. Comparing "high-involvement" teachers (those who reach out more often and in more ways) with "low-involvement" teachers, Epstein found that high-involvement teachers were more successful in involving parents, regardless of socioeconomic level (1986). But when initial overtures are met with resistance or nonresponsiveness, teachers' willingness to continue reaching out may suffer. In one instance, a student teacher sent a note home indicating that the parent would receive a phone call that evening. When the call came through, "[T]he mother yelled at the teacher and hung up the phone. The next morning the mother came into the classroom, screaming that she did not want to be disturbed at home and complaining that her daughter had been treated unfairly" (Winkelman, 1999, p. 81). It's clear that the mother did not regard the teacher's call as a positive action. In collectivistic cultures, a personal relationship is prerequisite to communication, and face-to-face communication — not the more impersonal telephone — is the norm. Lack of understanding of these cultural differences may have caused this problem.

More than information about what it takes to help their children succeed, parents may need to feel welcome in the school (Chavkin & Williams, 1993). In the Metropolitan Life survey mentioned earlier, "minority" parents reported that they were intimidated by the school's staff and institutional structure, that they felt awkward about approaching teachers (cited in Chavkin, 1989). Again, the problem may be a conflict between the bureaucratic impersonality of the school culture and the personal style of communication valued by parents from collectivistic cultural backgrounds.

Cultural differences can lead to entirely different perceptions of a single communicative act. A message intended to be neutral or even welcoming may be perceived as hostile. For example, even the customary "Please report to the principal's office before visiting your child's classroom" sign may seem unwelcoming or even punitive to a parent unfamiliar with the usual protocol of U.S. schools. In fact, from the collectivistic perspective, such a sign might be seen as creating a divide between parent and child. Consider other signs that convey important messages that are, unfortunately, rather negative: "No weapons on campus," "Drug-free zone," "No one allowed on campus without a pass." How many schools have signs that say: "Welcome Families"? Some do, of course, but all schools could benefit from examining the signs they post and evaluating their tone and impact on family members who visit their campuses.

Conflicting Expectations of Students

Conflicting expectations of students may remain misunderstood and stand in the way of constructive home-school relations. A study on child rearing beliefs of immigrant parents from Cambodia, Mexico, the Philippines, and Vietnam, as well as native-born Anglo-American and Mexican-American parents, showed that "Anglo-American parents valued autonomy and creativity more than did other parents. Immigrant parents valued conformity to external standards more than did the American-born parents" (Okagaki & Sternberg, 1993, p. 49). These values influence children's school behavior and teachers' evaluations of them. When parents have child-rearing goals different from those of the dominant society, their children are evaluated less favorably by teachers and tests (Okagaki & Sternberg, 1993).

How are we to understand these differences? A dangerous but common conclusion from such data is that one form of parenting must be superior to another when it comes to producing high-achieving children. But such a judgment of parental inadequacy does not take into account the positive values of group responsibility and social harmony that Latino immigrant parents are inculcating in their children. Why not instead conclude that schools are failing to capitalize on the strengths of children and failing to take responsibility for helping to resolve culture-based conflicts that children and families may encounter? After all, these values of helping, sharing, and respect are espoused — if less emphasized — by schools. At the very least, schools should recognize that undermining home values is not fruitful and help parents and children understand the dominant culture values to ease their transition into a new culture. The unnecessary damage of this one-sided perspective is reflected in a comment made by Mrs. Amada Pérez:

> I remember going through it [the conflict] as a child — as an immigrant child — and trying to become… to understand this system. And in my family it ended up where the school was right and the teachers were right, and their value became more important… and because of that many of my brothers just stopped communicating completely with my father, because he represented the bad, the wrong way, and that was hard.

QUESTIONING ASSUMPTIONS

There is little doubt that many schools genuinely want to involve parents more in their children's education. But the assumptions schools make about *how* parents should be involved are rarely questioned, and if "non-mainstream" parents are to be effectively engaged, these assumptions need to be examined. Schools seem to assume that appropriate ways to involve parents in their children's education are to offer advice on parenting, to encourage parents to volunteer in classrooms, to give guidance about how parents can help with schoolwork at home, and (less often) to recruit and train parents to take a leadership role in the school.

The usual approach assumes that schools need to reach out to parents and guide their involvement. It is based on the belief that schools know what parents need to know — how to provide a home environment that will support a good student, how to help with homework, how to discipline the child, and how to take a leadership role, including what aspects of schooling to take leadership in. Parents seem to agree that it *is* the school's responsibility to initiate the interchange (see Dauber & Epstein, 1993; Goldenberg & Gallimore, 1995; Chavkin & Williams, 1993). Research with immigrant Latino parents suggests that they appreciate teachers' efforts to involve them in their children's education. Yet there is a one-way quality in a high proportion of schools' efforts that virtually forecloses parent input about what kinds of workshops they would consider useful, for example, or how they would like to help their children. Of course, home-school *two-way* communication is desirable in *any* community; but it may be even more crucial in settings where the culture of school is different from the culture of home. The school cannot afford to assume it understands what parents want for their children or why they choose to participate or not in various activities. Ironically, immigrant parents' tendency to defer to the authority of the school may mean that the school has to make an exceptionally conscious and concerted effort to learn from parents. This need not be so difficult, as will be seen through some of the teachers' examples in Chapter 4.

LOOKING BEYOND DEMOGRAPHICS
TO INTERPERSONAL PROCESSES

If some parents tend to be less responsive to the activities schools design to encourage their involvement, this need not stymie school efforts to be more inclusive. Much of the research has focused on "status variables" like ethnic group membership or socioeconomic status. Other research has shown, however, that when schools shift their focus to "process variables," such as how parents make decisions and choices, they can enhance parent involvement (see Goldenberg & Gallimore, 1995; Hoover-Dempsey & Sandler, 1997). That means schools need to understand (1) what parents want for their children (and how that overlaps with what schools want for children); (2) what roles parents are comfortable in assuming with their children; (3) how competent parents feel to take on the tasks the school demands; (4) what kinds of invitations to parents succeed in getting their participation; and (5) what other kinds of roles (such as parent leader) parents may be willing to take, depending on the mechanisms and structures schools offer for them to participate. All of these pieces of cross-cultural understanding have been discussed above. The sections below offer additional guidelines and examples related to engaging parents successfully.

Identifying Appropriate Ways for Families to Help

In their review of family partnerships with schools, Connors and Epstein (1995) examined what parents do to support children's education. They acknowledge that parents are usually left on their own, drawing upon their own experiences, to figure out how to best support their children's learning in school. Consider how different this must be for parents from another country, with limited formal education compared to U.S.-born middle-class families with high school or college educations.

The Connors and Epstein review focuses on literacy-related parenting practices, homework-related practices, and influences on college and career plans. In each of these cases, suggestions are made about how parents can help children succeed in school. For example, parents are urged to provide a language-rich environment at home, including time for reading practice, modeling the reading and writing process, and making reading pleasant and enjoyable. However, limited literacy in a first language or in English will greatly hamper the ability of parents to be "teachers" for their children. Likewise, helping children with homework assumes that parents understand the concepts themselves. When parents have been taught math facts by rote, they may be ineffective in helping their children learn via deductive reasoning (Goldenberg & Gallimore, 1995).

One *Bridging Cultures* teacher developed a technique for practicing homework in small groups, initially with her guidance. Several children would discuss the homework without writing down any answers, thus affording them time to review concepts from class and to get clarification from the group on the questions and the answers. The children were still required to complete the homework at home, but they were not dependent on help at home to do so. This practice increased the rate of homework return from very low to nearly 100% (Rothstein-Fisch, Greenfield, & Trumbull, 1999).

Although parents do value academic growth, especially literacy, immigrants from Mexico and Central America may not provide experiences in the home that promote text-based literacy (Goldenberg & Gallimore, 1995). Indeed, in some homes of families in her study, according to Valdés (1996), the only printed material available was in the form of notes from school. Parents may read to their children but not ask children to respond to text the way dominant culture parents do (e.g., answering questions about what happened when, guessing what might happen next, talking about their thoughts on the story). The value of reading to children may be seen as building family unity or mainly as a way to pass on moral lessons. Younger children may not be introduced to print in the same ways as dominant culture children, who often enter school knowing the alphabet and how to spell their names (Goldenberg & Gallimore, 1995).

Educators should not draw the conclusion that it is impractical to continue to send children home with homework. However, they do need to learn about what goes on at home. For example, the frequent request to set aside a quiet study place may be unrealistic to a family living with eight other people in a garage or small apartment. The social closeness engendered by these living conditions may be perfectly natural and desirable to the occupants until the school request suggests that there is something wrong with the arrangement.

Understanding the Influence of Parents' Experiences with Schooling

When immigrant parents or those rooted strongly in "non-mainstream" cultures do try to comply with school requests to help their children with homework or engage in tutorial activities, they will likely use their own school experiences as a basis for understanding what to do — with mixed success (Delgado-Gaitan, 1992; Goldenberg & Gallimore, 1995). Teaching methods in their countries of origin may be quite different from those of the school their child attends. They may consequently focus on drill when critical thinking is called for. They may stress penmanship when quick and accurate computation is called for. As Delgado-Gaitan points out, to succeed in getting parents to provide certain kinds of home environments for learning, schools need to understand the influences that contribute to the ways parents participate in their children's education. She notes that these include "the cultural group identity, parents' educational background, their socioeconomic conditions, and the parents' knowledge about the school" (Delgado-Gaitan, 1992, p. 513).

In some settings, historical relations between parents or community and school make parent involvement in the schools particularly troublesome. A prior (and sometimes continuing) history of discrimination, such as experienced by American Indian, Alaska Native, Pacific Island, and Mexican peoples, whose nations were invaded, colonized or conquered, is a formidable barrier to harmonious parent inclusion in the schools (Lipka, Mohatt, & The Ciulistet Group, 1998; Onikama, Hammond, & Koki, 1998). The memory of forced removal to boarding schools far from home and community is still fresh in the minds of a great many parents and grandparents of the current generation of American Indian students. Knowledge of such history is important to understanding how some parents approach schools.

The Need to Obtain Key Information

Because of these possible differences, when teachers and parents are setting out joint goals in a parent-teacher conference, a teacher cannot assume that suggested literacy activities for the home will be carried out in the way expected. Instead, it behooves the teacher to find out what kinds of activities the parent is comfortable with and build on those. The teacher may want to ask the parent to describe what his or her own schooling experiences were like. (See Chapter 5 this volume for suggestions on how to do this.) And if parents are going to be asked to participate in homework activities, they need to be offered a range of ways to do so (Goldenberg & Gallimore, 1995). Sometimes older siblings, more familiar with U.S. schools than immigrant parents, are an important resource for homework help.

As suggested, careful attention to the kinds of roles parents want to take on is very important. We know that parents *do* want to support their children's school success; understanding their cultural values and own educational experiences provides clues as to how this motivation can be put into practice. The research on immigrant Latino families suggests that supervising academic homework is not the most likely or productive route for parents to take. However, some of the *Bridging Cultures* teachers *have* found ways to engage immigrant Latino parents in support of academic work (see examples in Chapter 4, this volume).

Parents can serve as sources of cultural knowledge about the community, but schools need to provide them mechanisms to do so. Schools must recognize that parent involvement activities are not just opportunities for schools to transmit knowledge to parents, but for parents to educate teachers and administrators as well (Allexsaht-Snider, 1992). The first step is to assume that useful knowledge resides in the community (see Dauber & Epstein, 1993; Moll & Greenberg, 1991; Seeley, 1993; Simich-Dudgeon, 1993). The next step is for educators to become "ethnographers," in effect eliciting information about their cultures from the parents of the children they teach, as well as from paraprofessional aides and other community members.

FINDING COMMON GROUND BETWEEN HOME AND SCHOOL

The *Bridging Cultures Project* seeks not only to understand the sources of cross-cultural conflict, but to identify ways to resolve or even prevent those conflicts. The researchers and teachers who have collaborated on this project are all interested in strategies that promote understanding and harmony in the classroom and between home and school. A continuing focus of the project is to identify examples that demonstrate how common ground can be reached through a variety of home-school connections.

Recognizing Continuities

Our emphasis on understanding cultural differences in no way implies common ground can't be found. Goldenberg and Gallimore, reflecting on ten years of research with immigrant Latino families, stress the "many continuities between the families and schools, often overlooked by teachers and school administrators and sometimes by researchers focused on identifying cultural differences and discontinuities to account for the differential achievement of Latino children with immigrant backgrounds" (1995, p. 197). Such observations serve both as a warning and as a beacon of optimism. On the one hand, we should not fall into the trap of using cultural differences as an excuse for low achievement. On the other hand, if we can use our cultural understanding to find common ground, there is no reason students cannot participate fully and successfully in the U.S. educational system and still maintain their home culture (see also Banks, 1995).

Taking a Constructive Stance

Perhaps the first step in the quest for common ground is actually an awareness or a realization. When teachers recognize how their own ways of thinking about child development and schooling are shaped by a particular cultural perspective, they can more easily begin to regard parents as sources of knowledge about a different perspective. A stance that reflects a respect for the "funds of knowledge" that are present in children's communities is critical to the process of cross-cultural understanding (Moll & Greenberg, 1991). As one European-American *Bridging Cultures* teacher commented: "I have a whole different perspective on culture and how it affects the decisions I made as a teacher. I see that my actions are culturally-bound also." In the next chapter, we apply this insight to the cross-cultural parent-teacher conference.

Questions for Reflection and Research

1. Why should schools do the reaching out to parents and not vice versa? What obstacles make it difficult for parents to initiate contact with schools?
2. Think about your school and specifically your classroom. Identify something you are doing or could be doing to make families feel more welcome at school.
3. How would you handle homework help for children whose parents have limited English literacy or limited literacy in general?
4. What are some of the informal ways you interact with parents? Can you think of other opportunities for informal interaction that you could cultivate?
5. Does your school have a parent/family resource center? If not, why not help start one?

Further Reading

Chavkin, N. F. (Ed.), (1993). *Families and schools in a pluralistic society.* New York: State University of New York Press.

Dauber, S. L., & Epstein, J. L. (1993). Parents' attitudes and practices of involvement in inner-city elementary and middle schools. In N. F. Chavkin (Ed.), *Families and schools in a pluralistic society* (pp. 53-71). New York: NY: State University of New York Press.

Delgado-Gaitan, C. (1994). Sociocultural change through literacy: Toward the empowerment of families. In B. Ferdman, R.M. Weber, & A. Ramirez (Eds.), *Literacy across languages and cultures*. New York: SUNY Press.

Nieto, S. (1996). *Affirming diversity: The sociopolitical context of multicultural education* (2nd Ed.). White Plains, NY: Longman.

Trumbull, E., Rothstein-Fisch, C., & Greenfield, P.M. (2000). Bridging Cultures: *New approaches that work*. Knowledge Brief, San Francisco: WestEd.

chapter 3

The Cross-Cultural Parent-Teacher Conference

We start first with defining the "cross-cultural conference" and discuss the kinds of problems that arise in such conferences. Then we move to concrete strategies for improving cross-cultural conferences, including ideas from the literature on cross-cultural communication and successful practices used by *Bridging Cultures* teachers. We stress that good practices *evolve* over time on the basis of new thinking and understanding and that they will be effective to the degree that they reflect the particular context of the school and community. Therefore, readers should not assume that the specific strategies described here will suit their own needs. We hope, however, that the examples in this book do stimulate creative thinking about how to maximize the effectiveness of parent-teacher conferences.

Table 3.1 presents some reflections of *Bridging Cultures* teachers on how the project has changed them. By sharing their representative comments, we hope to set the stage for talking about a specific and common element of home-school communication, the parent-teacher conference. In fact, changes in teachers' thinking were the foundation for considerable analysis and innovation regarding parent-teacher conferences. From these reflections, it is possible to get a sense of the depth of teachers' commitment to approaching their students and families with greater cultural sensitivity. This commitment shows up in their innovations related to parent-teacher conferences.

Table 3.1
Comments of *Bridging Cultures* Teachers

"I am much more aware of how strongly the collectivist model is ingrained in my Latino students and how strongly the individualistic model is ingrained in our curriculum, teaching methods, and society."

"The framework has given me a greater understanding of why my kids tend to work together automatically."

"Every day I will be much more understanding and tolerant of my students' need to help each other and their families."

"The framework changed my view and understanding of the parents' actions and views."

"As an immigrant from Mexico myself, I can see how I have had to fight my own collectivistic upbringing to be successful in U.S. schools. Those of us who jumped from one orientation to another made the leap without even knowing it! Now we need to tap our own cultural knowledge for the sake of our students."

WHAT IS A CROSS-CULTURAL
PARENT-TEACHER CONFERENCE?

A cross-cultural parent-teacher conference is *not* necessarily a conference in which the teacher is from one ethnic group and the parents are from another. We focus on culture not as an ethnic label but as an internal value system. In this view, the cross-cultural parent-teacher conference is one in which the teacher has internalized and operates from the perspective of the individualistic values of the school system, while the parents have internalized and operate from a contrasting set of cultural values. The teacher's cultural values generate one set of priorities for child development, while the parents' cultural values generate another. Our research indicates that a cross-cultural parent-teacher conference can sometimes take place between parents and teachers from the same ethnic group. This can happen because teachers, in the process of obtaining their education, are taught instructional methods based on a single set of (dominant culture) values.

Although the parent-teacher conference is just one strategy schools use to engage parents, it is a pivotal exchange that deserves careful attention for several reasons. First, the parent-teacher conference is almost a "mini-laboratory" for discovering how different values shape different understandings of children's development (and different goals for schooling), creating problems in parent-teacher communication. Second, we have first-hand data on cross-cultural parent-teacher conferences, along with a simple method for analyzing parent-teacher communication that others can use to monitor the success of the conference (Greenfield, Quiroz, & Raeff, 2000). Finally, *Bridging Cultures* teachers have urged us to address this topic because of their own concerns and frustrations, as well as the recognition that other teachers — particularly new teachers — can benefit from what they have learned.

The *Bridging Cultures* teachers' perspective has shifted from regarding these conferences chiefly as opportunities for parent education to viewing them as an opportunity for mutual understanding and true communication. Indeed, they have experimented with the entire format of parent-teacher conferences, as we will discuss in the second half of this chapter. Of course, the teachers *always* saw the conference as a two-way learning opportunity, but they have a new sense of what that means. In the past, they may have asked parents about important events going on in the family (the birth of a baby, absence or illness of a parent, and the like). However, now, because they have more insight into parents' collectivistic points of view about child development and education, they understand why such questions are so important and must *precede* academic issues if the teachers are to establish rapport with these parents.

THE TRADITION OF PARENT-TEACHER CONFERENCES

Parent-teacher conferences are a staple in the repertoire of public school practices. A recent study of 900 U.S. elementary schools showed that 92% scheduled school-wide parent-teacher conferences; most of the remaining schools likely provided for scheduling parent-teacher meetings at the discretion of teachers (Carey, Lewis, & Farris, 1998). The study showed that parents were more likely to attend a parent conference than any other school-wide event open to them. Certainly, parents and teachers do have other opportunities to meet and discuss mutual concerns and interests at activities such as back-to-school nights, open houses, special assemblies, and even sports events. However, the parent-teacher conference is usually the one formal occasion when parents and teacher meet alone face-to-face for a designated amount of time, to focus on a single student. (However, this is not the only possible or always the most successful format, as we shall see.)

Parent-teacher conferences are widely accepted as an opportunity for parents and teachers to share their perceptions about a student's school performance and come to some understanding of what the student's needs are. Frequently used to explain report card grades, these meetings are typically scheduled in conjunction with the completion of a grading period. The conference is often used to "emphasize the parents' role in the education of the child and ways the teacher can assist them" and to provide resources and materials the parents can use at home (Moles, 1996, p. 22).

RESEARCH ON CROSS-CULTURAL PARENT-TEACHER CONFERENCES

Greenfield, Quiroz, and Raeff videotaped nine parent-teacher conferences between immigrant parents from Mexico and El Salvador and their children's European-American teacher. The classroom was a combination third and fourth grade. The conferences were naturally-occurring, not specially scheduled for the study. As might be expected, these parent-teacher meetings showed instances of both harmonious and discordant communication. However, there was considerably more discord than harmony in the "social construction" of children by teacher and parents, i.e., in the ways each envisioned an "ideal child" in the classroom or family. Analysis of the communication patterns of the nine conferences revealed that far more often than not parent and teacher disagreed on goals for children. For example, the teacher was more interested in discussing cognitive skills, while parents were more interested in talking about social behavior (cf., Chapter 1 this volume).

Parent-teacher conferences are a real opportunity for teachers and parents to learn from each other. Yet, for many reasons, they often turn out to be more of a *missed* opportunity. Teachers may feel pressured to cover too many issues in a conference, and even when they have smaller classes, it seems there is never enough time. When teacher and parent come from different linguistic and cultural backgrounds, the conference may be complicated by problems in communication even when a translator is present. But the problems often are actually "below" the conversational level, in the kinds of assumptions each person is making about what is most important — for example, the individual child or the family unit or social or academic development.

CULTURE AND COMMUNICATION
IN THE PARENT-TEACHER CONFERENCE

Sources of Miscommunication

Parents' expectations of their children, and of the school, guide how they interpret what the teacher says and vice versa. When there is "miscommunication," it is often not the words that are said that cause the problem, but the (usually unconscious) expectations underlying the words that present stumbling blocks. As we have said, when parents and teachers share common values, they are likely to hold shared assumptions about the goals of child development. This underlying agreement leads to a similar set of expectations for the child. When the participants do not share the same values, there is a real risk of misunderstanding in the parent-teacher conference. It is important to realize that when parent and teacher cannot come to common understanding, the outcome is not *neutral* (i.e., simply a failure to communicate): in fact, parents and teachers alike have lamented that it is a highly *negative* experience for both (Greenfield, Raeff, & Quiroz, 1998; Greenfield, Quiroz, & Raeff, 2000).

Diagnosing and Repairing
Communication Problems in the Conference

It is not unusual for an immigrant Latino parent and a teacher to complain about a lack of communication with each other, but often neither understands what is really causing the problem. Here is a technique for shaping parent-teacher communication that works for everyone's needs, the teacher's, parent's, and ultimately the child's. In order to recognize conflicts, the teacher goes beyond conversational content to look at the interactional processes between herself and parents. The teacher can monitor the success of the conversation by considering the following questions:

- Does the parent ratify (validate/acknowledge) a topic you have brought up by verbal or nonverbal means?
- Does the parent verbally elaborate on the same topic you have introduced?
- Does the parent confirm a specific comment or observation you have made?

See Table 3.2 for examples.

Table 3.2 Discourse Examples from Actual Conferences

A. Parent ratification of a topic introduced by teacher
  1. Teacher: Also I hope that she has, has time to read orally
  2. Mother: (Nodding and smiling) Ahhuh.
  3. Teacher: and also silent every night
  4: Mother: Ahhuh.

B. Parent elaboration of a topic introduced by teacher
  (continuation of conversation above)
  5. Teacher: with you orally and with her silent in the bed for a book
     which she has an interest
  6. Mother: Ahhuh. She took out from the library. How many? Seven?

C. Parents' confirmation of teacher's comment
  7. Teacher: (pointing to report card): Takes pride in her work. Most
     of the time her work is neat, but I'd like her to work a li: :ttle bit
     harder on trying to make sure that just − not perfect, bu[t as]=
  8. Father: Yeah
  9. Teacher: As neat as possible
  10. Mother: Yeah, a little bit
  11. Teacher: Yeah, a little neater.
  12. Mother: A little bit neater.
  13. Teacher: Yeah, work on your handwriting a little bit.
  14. Mother: Yeah, she could improve it.

D. Lack of parent ratification of a topic introduced by teacher
  15. Teacher: She's doing great. She's doing beautifully in
     English and in reading. And in writing, and in speaking.
  16. Father: Looks down at lap.

E. Changing of teacher's topic by parent (continuation of
  conversation above)
  17. Teacher: It's wonderful.
  18. Father: (turning to point to younger son) The same,
     this guy, h[e]
  19. Teacher: (interrupting, with shrill tone) [G]o: :d!
  20. Father: [He can] write =
  21. Teacher: (cutting him off) He can write in English?
  22. Father: = well, his name.

Key to linguistic notations:
  : : double colon symbolizes lengthening of a syllable
  − dash indicates being cut off by next speaker
  = pair of equal signs (one after earlier utterance and one before later
     utterance) indicates later followed earlier with no discernible silence
     between
  [ ] brackets indicate material said simultaneously

(From Greenfield, Quiroz, & Raeff, 2000. Note: Examples A, B, and C are
from one conference; examples D and E from another.)

Ratification, elaboration, and confirmation are all signs that the parent is in agreement with the teacher about the importance of what he or she is saying and that the parent agrees with the teacher's interpretation of the facts. In such a "cooperative" conversation, parent and teacher are on the same wavelength. Of course, we must remember that communication is a *reciprocal* process: Both teacher and parent should be introducing topics and responding to the other's comments. Consequently, a teacher might want to reverse the roles in the questions above and ask:

- Do I ratify (validate) a topic the parent has brought up by verbal or nonverbal means?
- Do I elaborate on the same topic the parent has introduced (verbally)?
- Do I confirm a specific comment or observation the parent has made (with either a verbal or nonverbal response)?

Instances of Conversational Harmony

In examples A and B in Table 3.2, teacher and parent seem to be in agreement that reading orally and silently are important activities for the child. They may not have the same reasons for believing so, but there is no conversational discord at this point. In example C (taken from the same parent-teacher conference), we see apparent agreement on a learning goal: the improvement of the child's handwriting. Note how harmonious the conversation is when the teacher makes a criticism about the child's handwriting and says it could be neater. (Recall the discussion of praise versus criticism in Chapter 1 this volume.)

Instances of Discord

On the other hand, if a parent does not acknowledge what the teacher has said, becomes silent, or actually changes the topic, he or she probably either does not agree with the teacher or does not think the teacher's topic is all that important. Such conversation could be characterized as "uncooperative." Something is clearly going awry. The examples labeled "D" and "E" in Table 3.2 show a striking failure in communication. The father does not pick up on the teacher's desire to talk about the child's academic success, while the teacher seems uncomfortable discussing the academic merits of another family member. The researchers explain:

> The father shows discomfort when the teacher recognizes his daughter as outstanding, as she does in Turn 1; he responds by looking down at his lap in

Turn 2. According to our analysis, her recognition may threaten the collectiv-istic goal of integrating each child as an equal contributing part of the family group. Hence, when the teacher symbolically constructs his daughter as an outstanding individual learner, the father implicitly *reconstructs* her as a normative part of the family group by equating her academic skills to those of her younger brother (Turns 4, 6, and 8) (Greenfield, Quiroz, & Raeff, 2000, p. 101).

Another videotaped parent-teacher conference reveals cross-cultural con-flict around the issue of verbal expression. The teacher has been talking about how well the child is using language to express herself and ask questions. When she asks the father toward the end of the conference whether he has any ques-tions, he asks, "How is she doing? She don't talk too much?" (Greenfield, Quiroz, & Raeff, 2000, p. 102). In encouraging the child to talk more in class, the teacher is promoting behavior that is positively valued in school but negatively valued in the child's home community, where respectful silence is the desired norm. This creates a conflict for both parent and child, and this type of conflict has the potential to alienate children from their parents (or from the school). "Similarly, it could alienate parents from their children or from their children's school" (Green-field, Quiroz, & Raeff, 2000, p. 102; see also "Oral Expression versus Respect for Authority," Chapter 1).

Successful Monitoring

When the parent ratifies what the teacher is saying, elaborates on the teacher's comments or confirms them, the communication is going well. Likewise, the teacher should note whether she is responding to parents' topics adequately. Awareness of the collectivistic perspective and possible points of conflict, as outlined in Chapter 1, may enable the communication to get back on track. For example, the teacher could have started the conference by acknowledging the younger son and perhaps even the father's family as a whole.

It is not worthwhile for the teacher to pursue the topic she has initiated when the parent has become disconnected from the dialogue. Yet, this situation can be very difficult for a teacher. For example, it can be highly frustrating for a teacher who defines her mission as the academic accomplishment of her pupils to commu-nicate with parents who value social comportment more highly (See "Cognitive versus Social Skills," Chapter 1). What can be done to find common ground in such a case? Since the difference is one of priorities more than an either-or choice, one pragmatic strategy is for the teacher to simply change the order of topics and deal with the parent's priority first (social comportment, in this particular example). Once parents are reassured that the child is behaving correctly in class, they may be more open to hearing about strictly academic matters. In any case, it is important for the teacher to keep in mind that the goal is to find common ground, not to reform parents' notions of education or child-rearing.

Other Cultural Contexts

Although the conversational examples we have used here pertain to immigrant Latino parents and a European-American teacher, the strategies for monitoring a conversation can be used with other cultural combinations. Of course, to understand why conversational problems occur, it is necessary to know something about the backgrounds of both parents and teachers. In the case of many immigrant and American Indian groups, parents may bring collectivistic assumptions about the child into the individualistic context of the school in general and the parent-teacher conference in particular. There is no sure-fire formula for successful communication, and it is impossible to anticipate every conversational twist and turn. However, if the teacher is able to recognize conversational breakdown, he or she can take steps to investigate why it may be occurring and remedy it.

USING CULTURAL KNOWLEDGE
TO ENHANCE COMMUNICATION

In Chapter 5 we will discuss how a teacher who does *not* come from the same culture as a particular child or family can become an *ethnographer* — one who learns directly from her students and parents about their cultures. Teacher aides (or paraprofessionals) are also an important source of cultural knowledge. In many schools, they are the only adults who understand the cultures and speak the languages of students from groups that have recently emigrated. Even when the language of students is widely spoken, a paraprofessional who comes from the particular background of students and their families can bring critical cultural understanding into the realm of school, if he or she is shown the appropriate interest and respect.

One of us (Quiroz) developed the suggestions that follow, from the perspective of a cultural insider. As a parent who emigrated from Mexico in adulthood and later became a teacher and researcher, she is able to reflect on her own first-hand experience through the theoretical lens of individualism and collectivism. She draws on her cultural knowledge, as well as her experience on both sides of the parent-teacher conference.

Fostering a Comfortable and Respectful Conversational Tone

There are steps teachers can take to make the conversational tone of parent-teacher communication sensitive to parents with collectivistic backgrounds. In general, conversation should be kept as informal as possible. A certain amount of social "small talk" is expected. But informality does not necessarily mean familiarity. As with many languages, Spanish makes the distinction between a familiar and a polite form of the pronoun "you." (Note that English seems to be suited to a less hierarchical, more egalitarian society by its lack of such a distinction.) Spanish-speaking teachers need to remember that it is advisable to use the pronoun "*usted*" (the polite form of "you") and not "*tu*" (the familiar form) when addressing a parent. This practice will maintain the appropriate conversational status between teacher and parent. The use of "*usted*" conveys respect, but it also maintains a certain social distance (Brown, 1957). Although the relationship between teacher and parent may become cordial and in some ways personal, it is probably inadvisable to lapse into using "*tu*," no matter how natural that feels.

Using Indirect Questions

Teachers may need to use several prompts to get the information they need, and a less direct approach to information-gathering is likely to be more successful. Teachers often want to establish joint goals with parents for children. However, for Latino parents of collectivistic orientations, discussing their children's goals is a very sensitive and intimate matter. A question-and-answer format may give an undesired impression of coldness, as though teacher and parent are putting together an impersonal business plan for the child. Also, indirectness is considered more polite than directness in conversation (Lustig & Koester, 1999).

Rather than ask if the student has a designated time and space for doing homework, the teacher may make an observation such as, "Sometimes parents say it's hard to seat their children at a specific place to do homework or study because some of us live in small places and have other people around us all the time." (People with an essentially collectivistic orientation do not necessarily seek private space even if they have the room to do so. It may seem natural for children to be completing tasks in the presence of many other family members and the concept of needing privacy to do so alien.) If parents are faced with a similar problem, they may be relieved to hear that it has been voiced by someone else and less embarrassed to talk about it. The experiences of other parents, rather than direct prescriptions by the teacher, can be used as a source of suggestions for solutions to problems. This approach gives the teacher the chance to acknowledge other parents' problem-solving strategies and help parents without embarrassing them.

It also situates the parent as part of a group of parents rather than as an individual. Conversation of this nature reflects the kind of respect one would expect to be shown between teachers and parents in a collectivistic culture. It can begin to foster in the parent a feeling of acceptance and increased comfort with the teacher and the school.

Recognizing Collectivistic Values

Because modesty is valued by many immigrant Latino families, teachers may want to talk about student achievements in the context of the classroom group and emphasize how such achievements are socially valued. (See the earlier discussion of "Praise versus Criticism" in Chapter 1.) For example, if a child is especially good at critical thinking, explaining how that ability contributes to the class's performance or even to the community is probably more pleasing to the parents, and perhaps to the child, than hearing how much the child has excelled in comparison to other children. Parents feel especially comfortable in hearing about areas where additional effort is needed for the child to come up to group norms (Greenfield, Quiroz, & Raeff, 2000). In a collection of interviews with high-achieving Chicanos, Gandara has documented the isolating effects of such achievement. Being identified as "gifted" or "high-achieving" in comparison to their classmates and deviating from their group of ethnic reference was bearable for them only because of the acknowledgment of the contribution that their achievement brought back to the group (Gandara, 1995).

In forming relationships with students' families, it is appropriate for a teacher to explain the standard expectations of the school (e.g., as measured through report cards and grades) as separate and sometimes distinct from the shared goals that teacher and parents may hold for a child. Parents doubtless want to ensure that their children succeed in school and do not want to undermine their children's chances, nor do they want to be noncompliant with the school. Nevertheless, their desire to comply may conflict with their collectivistic values in some cases — putting them in a terrible bind. The earlier example of the father's discomfort when one of his children was praised as outstanding to the exclusion of others reflects a conflict between the school's values and the family's goal of enculturating children to fit in rather than stand out. We question whether this bind is inevitable. Is a completely individualistic orientation to goals necessary? Could goals not be framed in terms of importance to family and community as well?

Communicating a Message of Caring

Subtle cues can help transmit a message of caring and appreciation for another culture's valuing of family ("familism"). When talking about a child with that child's parents, a teacher can create a bond of trust through the use of the right pronoun. As we suggested earlier, schools or teachers may not realize that for some parents the use of the exclusive pronouns "I" and "you" conveys a sense of separation between teacher and parents (recall the hypothetical workshop invitation to parents mentioned in Chapter 1). In talking about the child, it is appropriate to use "we," to communicate that teacher and family are a team — especially when talking about a child's problems or goals. In such a case, teacher and parents both have knowledge about common goals and problems and need to work as a team to address them. Using the pronoun "we" makes it clear to the parents that the teacher has something in common with them and that they all share responsibility for ensuring the child's successful performance in school. This stance is compatible with the collectivistic orientation toward group membership.

Cultivating Empathy

We do not mean to suggest that teachers should memorize a set of rules for conversing with immigrant Latino parents or anyone from a collectivistic culture. Rather, we want to encourage teachers to learn enough about a collectivistic orientation to acquire a sense of how a parent from such a background might think and feel, and to come to understand the expectations such a parent might have of the teacher and the school. Understanding the potential differences between a collectivistic culture at home and the culture of the "mainstream" at school can promote empathy, something that is far more helpful than prescriptions about question-asking or pronoun usage.

Knowledge of how individualism and collectivism operate also helps teachers to adapt their interaction style to parents' styles. For example, Latino parents with more years of formal schooling or who have been in the U.S. for several years (and have had older children in the school) may be more comfortable with a conference that focuses on academic achievement. The key is to open the door to understanding differences and to shape conferences accordingly. One conference style does not fit all.

IMPROVING PARENT-TEACHER CONFERENCES

Bridging Cultures teachers, like other teachers, have struggled with the logistics of parent-teacher conferences. These conferences are usually too short; 15 to 20 minutes per child is often all that is allocated within the school schedule, severely limiting what can be covered. It could be argued that if the conference is to be used to forge cross-cultural understanding — when parents and teachers do not start off with the same assumptions about schooling and learning — even more time than usual is required. *Bridging Cultures* teachers have been experimenting with strategies for getting more time with parents. Some have extended the number of days they will stay after school for conferences in order to get at least half an hour with each set of parents. Teachers have suggested that conferences could be "tiered" so that kindergarten and first grade are at the same time, second and third, and so on. This might obviate the difficulties parents encounter when they have several children in a school and find themselves running from classroom to classroom or choosing which classroom to visit.

It is not always evident to teachers which innovations are culturally-appropriate and which are not. For instance, having children who have become proficient in English translate for their parents who have not seems practical on the surface. However, "[p]lacing children in a position of equal status with adults creates dysfunction within the family hierarchy" for Latino parents (Finders & Lewis, 1994, p. 52). A similar problem was recognized by the *Bridging Cultures* teachers when they had a chance to discuss student-led conferences together in one of the whole-group meetings. They realized that having students actually lead the conference would violate role norms. They agreed that it would probably be acceptable for the child to show the parent around the room and show examples of his or her work (e.g., in a portfolio). But the teacher should be taking the lead in discussing the child's progress, and then she or he and the parent(s) should jointly discuss what the child's needs are. Many districts have become enamored with student-led conferences, touting them as one way to promote student self-evaluation. But before they become more widely institutionalized, someone ought to raise questions about their appropriateness to families holding respect for elders as a cultural value.

Group Conferences

Two *Bridging Cultures* teachers have developed an alternative conference format that *is* culturally appropriate for their settings. They have found small-group conferences to be very successful with immigrant Latino parents. One, a kindergarten teacher, has brought parents together on the basis of their children's ability groups. Grouping resulted in considerable verbal interaction among parents. In each group, at least one parent was willing to talk, and that seemed to make other parents comfortable to participate as well. An upper elementary teacher did group conferences for the first time in the fall of 1998. Her account appears in the following box.

The new group format organized by the teacher appears to be well-liked, efficient, and culturally congruent. As a result, the school's principal asked the teacher to lead a school-wide staff-development session on her approach. Several teachers in her school are now experimenting with this format.

As *Bridging Cultures* teachers observe, immigrant Latino parents may feel more comfortable speaking in a group, with one parent's ideas stimulating another parent to comment or ask a question. The kindergarten teacher remarked that with group conferences the interaction is much more "give and take" and that she finds she does much less talking. Teachers get less burned out explaining the same thing over and over and can be more genuinely "present" to the experience. Perhaps most important, parents gain a sense of empowerment from the opportunity

GROUPS WORK BETTER FOR PARENTS AND TEACHER

I scheduled three group conferences on the "Pupil Free Day," two Spanish-speaking groups and one English-speaking group. I arranged the Spanish language groups when my paraprofessional aide could attend and assist in translation. For parents who were not able to attend during the day, I scheduled a separate time.

The parents sat in a circle with me and the children (including many siblings of the children in the class). The children presented their parents (mostly mothers) with a folder that contained test scores, report card, a parent tips list, and a booklet designed to help parents interpret test scores. I explained a simple way of understanding how the children's test results showed which academic areas were strong and which needed improvement. I discussed the report card and talked about how parents could help students at home. Students then escorted their parents and siblings to their desks to share and discuss their work portfolios. They also took their parents on a tour of the room to show their displayed work. This worked pretty smoothly, because I had helped the students prepare the previous week by role-playing the parts that would be taken by student and parent.

Parents seemed very pleased with the new approach to conferencing. A friendly, comfortable, and warm feeling came across during the conferencing. Many parents had questions that benefited the other parents. Parents' conferencing together lent a source of mutual support, like family members all supporting each other. This familial atmosphere aligns with a collectivistic model.

> I found the group conferencing to be relaxing for the parents. It was a less threatening environment than the individual conferencing style, with support and company lent by the other parents. This format elicited a group voice from the parents rather than an individual voice. It also represented a shift in the balance of power. My paraprofessional assisted in the translation of my commentary and the parents' questions and responses.
>
> I was able to meet with 22 out of 28 parents in the group format. For those who attended the group conferences, I also provided an opportunity during the hour following each conference for parents to ask private questions or set up a time for an individual conference. The remaining six parents were seen within the three-day conference period at another time (Quiroz, Greenfield, & Altchech, 1999).
>
> — Marie Altchech

to participate as part of a group. This is an innovation that might have value also for "mainstream" parents in order to help them develop a greater sense of community and a concern for the development and accomplishments of other people's children. It is important to find out from parents what they prefer, however. The group conference is an option, but it should not be automatically imposed on any set of parents any more than individual conferences or student-led conferences should be imposed without consideration for the particular cultural context.

Cross-Town Conferences

In districts where students may be bused clear across town, teachers are faced with the dilemma of how to connect with their parents. It may be logistically impractical or almost impossible for some of these parents to get to the school at the designated times for conferences — or at all. Some parents have several children who cannot easily be left at home, and dragging them along on public transportation for many miles is a hardship. Says Giancarlo Mercado, "For some of them, their job is watching babies, and they bring all of them to the home-school meeting." How could such a mother come to a conference in a school way beyond her own neighborhood? One teacher had 16 students bused in this past year, and he had to develop his own solution to the distance problem.

The account given by Mercado illustrates several points. One is the complexity of the lives of both parents and teachers: Interpretation of the motives and behaviors of either needs to be done on the basis of considerable information. It may not be feasible for all teachers in Mercado's position to take the steps he has, but his example underlines the possible payoff of such extraordinary effort. At the same time, we see why unflattering generalizations about parents' motives — when they don't participate in expected ways — can be terribly unfair. Mercado's strategies for connecting with parents reflect elements of both collectivism and

THE MOBILE CONFERENCE

Because we had additional room at our school last year, I suddenly had 16 students bused-in from East Hollywood — quite a distance from Venice, where I teach. I am a community style teacher, and it's important for me to have a strong rapport with the parents. I usually have a personal contact with many if not all of the parents at the beginning of the year — so I couldn't imagine what I was going to do. How was I going to meet the needs of the parents who lived outside of the local area? I like to begin the year with a formal assessment of each child, followed by a parent conference where we set mutual goals. This was going to be impossible. Parents who lived in East Hollywood simply weren't very likely to attend conferences in Venice! How was I going to include these parents in the goal-setting? Goals aren't much good without the agreement, feedback, and support of the parents.

I realized I had to go to them. So I took a day off from work (not easy to arrange, but possible) and went to their neighborhood. I was able to get a classroom in a year-round school that had some teachers off-track at the time. I scheduled all 16 parents between 7:30 and 4:30. I introduced myself, and they told me about themselves. We always start with chit-chat. I've been to all but three of the Latin American countries, so I can talk with them about places and foods. I ate lunch with some parents, looking for commonalities with the purpose of creating bonds. It takes the teacher off the pedestal. Parents might think, "He eats our food and knows our country. He has come over to our community to help make goals for our children."

Goals begin with what the parent feels the child needs. Usually it is reading, multiplication, ESL [English as a Second Language]. It's usually just what I think the child needs, too. We talk about a wide spectrum of things. We write the goals together and list strategies for achieving them. I use a piece of carbon paper so that we each end up with a final document. I set it up so that there's a list of all the areas to improve and a list of all the areas of strength. I do start with the strengths. I may mention "wonderful penmanship, wonderful helper, very athletic, enjoys science," and that I am happy to have their son or daughter in my class. Then we get into areas for improvement. The parents walk away with a copy of the paper.

Four months later I bring the original sheet to the next conference, and I start crossing out the goals that have been accomplished, so the parents can feel the progress. I just put a few goals on after some have been accomplished. Even when I have a phone conversation, I refer to the paper and jot down notes about the parents' backgrounds. For example, "This mother has no husband and five other children." When you have so many students you can't remember everything about the home situations, but it is so important to refer to it. I can ask, "Is your grandmother feeling better?" "I'm sorry. I heard about your mother passing away." It is more part of a family extension. It's not just academic. It's the whole child: academic, emotional, the family, all of that. Noting family details is an important part of the parent-teacher conference. It provides a reference point that is culturally relevant, honoring the family as a unit, while also understanding that the student is affected by all the elements within the family's multiple contexts.

Some parents have told me, and this is with a child in fourth-fifth grade, that their child has gone all five years without the parents' ever meeting his or her teachers. The child may have never been referred for assessment, yet children come to me unable to read or not having been tested for gifted programs. I'm shocked this year that two students have been recommended for special education as fifth graders!

So, back to the students from East Hollywood: Three times a year I take a day off to meet parents at the "home school" (the elementary school in their neighborhood). Some parents I meet a lot more if we can arrange for the bus company to let them ride to school with their children. They can go on field trips, or come to open house, or come for some culminating activity. This way they can stay the whole day and become part of the class. There's a problem for families with infants because the school bus company won't allow them to ride. So parents with very young children don't come unless they ride the public bus. These visits to the "home school," contacts with the bus company, and phone calls have helped me answer the question, "How am I going to get the feeling of community with my bused-in parents?" Yes, it takes effort, but they are making an effort, too. And I can't think of what our relationship would be like if I didn't meet them halfway.

— Giancarlo Mercado

individualism. He has not excised praise from his parent-teacher conferences (as some might be tempted to do in "applying the framework") but it's put into a context of "completed goals." In addition, he balances it with attention to goals for improvement; not only traveling across town, but sharing his personal knowledge of parents' home countries and cultures communicates his interest in their children and in them — in the family as a whole.

PUTTING THE PARENT-TEACHER CONFERENCE IN PROPER PERSPECTIVE

It is not realistic to expect the parent-teacher conference to serve more than a fraction of the need to communicate between home and school. Conferences should be just a small component of parent-teacher relations. *Bridging Cultures* teachers emphasize that teachers should not wait until conference time to begin establishing good communication and sharing information about report cards, school policies, and the like — along with eliciting information and perspectives from parents (see also Chavkin, 1989; Chrispeels, 1988). "There is groundwork to be laid long before the first conference," as Chavkin notes, "and follow-up to be done after the meeting" (Chavkin, 1989, p. 122). Successful communication must be nurtured through a whole variety of formal and informal interactions. Innovations in other forms of cross-cultural communication will be discussed in the next chapter.

Questions for Reflection and Research

1. If you are already a teacher, would you make any changes in your parent-teacher conferences after reading this chapter? If so, what would they be?
2. If you have not yet had parent-teacher conferences, how do you think you would design them to make immigrant Latino parents feel most comfortable?
3. What factors might you want to consider in planning culturally-appropriate conferences for your students' parents? How could you find out what parents would prefer?
4. What are the experiences of other teachers with parent-teacher conferences? Expand your own understanding by talking with others.

Further Reading

Greenfield, P.M., Quiroz, B., & Raeff, C. (2000). Cross-cultural conflict and harmony in the social construction of the child. In S. Harkness, C. Raeff, & C. M. Super (Eds.), *The social construction of the child: Nature and sources of variability. New directions in child psychology.* San Francisco: Jossey-Bass.

Quiroz, B., Greenfield, P. M., & Altchech, M. (1999). *Bridging Cultures* with a parent-teacher conference. *Educational Leadership*, 56(7), 68-70.

chapter 4

Learning What Works

In the course of the three *Bridging Cultures* workshops in the fall of 1996, participating teachers' own orientations shifted strongly from pure individualism toward collectivism, leaving them with a greater balance between the two value orientations (Rothstein-Fisch, Trumbull, Quiroz, & Greenfield, 1997). Their reflections, moreover, showed that they do not regard one orientation as superior to the other. In line with this new balance in their value systems, they found that adding elements of the collectivistic orientation created more harmony in their classrooms of immigrant Latino children. It also created a more "pro-social" atmosphere, something that is desperately needed by schools everywhere.

As demonstrated by the example of the parent-teacher conference innovation, the shift described above was evidenced in new ways of relating to parents. This chapter presents examples of changes teachers have made that strengthen parent-teacher relationships. All the educational practices we discuss involve a compromise between individualism and collectivism; they are not purely collectivistic. Schooling is, by its very nature, individualistic: for example, grades are given to individuals, not groups. Ways of interacting with parents have typically reflected the same individualistic values (as in the assumption that individual conferences are best). In developing more effective cross-cultural strategies, *Bridging Cultures* teachers have introduced collectivistic elements into existing practices. As we noted at the beginning of the *Guide*, the choice of the bridge metaphor reflects a recognition that both cultures are important. The strategies of the teacher-researchers discussed in the following pages are intended to help students, in particular, but also teachers and parents cross the bridge between the two orientations. As we have said, our working model of what makes for student success is a *bicultural* one. Students should not have to sacrifice their home-culture identities and their relationships with their families in order to succeed in school.

The most exciting aspect of the *Bridging Cultures Project* has been the dynamic nature of the change process. New understandings of the home culture and the value assumptions that many immigrant Latino families bring to school have led to spontaneous changes in teachers' feelings, beliefs, and practices. Despite the current emphasis in national and statewide reform efforts on changes in practice — and, more explicitly, changes in practice that lead to improved test scores — we should not underestimate the effect of changes in feelings and beliefs on relationships with children and families. As Ms. Altchech observed, "It's easy to rush to judgment about a parent who has not been able to get a child to school for a week... or about how children stay up late [and are tired in school the next day] ... because that's when they get to see their parents who come home late from work. It still may be possible to talk with the parent about getting the child to bed early whenever possible but recognize the reality of many children's situations." Many changes, both in the ways teachers understand families and in their practices have met with extremely positive reactions by students and parents. Most astonishing is how much easier these changes have made teaching and home-school relations. These positive outcomes, in turn, create more energy for further cross-cultural adaptations.

The last chapter considered parent-teacher conferences. The following pages offer other in-depth examples of strategies *Bridging Cultures* teachers have developed to (1) make classrooms and schools more welcome places for families, (2) promote bicultural proficiency, and (3) extend opportunities for parent-teacher interaction so that genuine home-school relationships can be built. Some first-person accounts from the teacher-researchers present ways they have altered their practices related to parent involvement and the results they have seen.

Meeting Families Halfway:
Allowing Impromptu Family Visits to the Classroom

Bridging Cultures teacher-researchers have consciously become more flexible in their interactions with parents. First-grade teacher Pearl Saitzyk used to find it inconsiderate of parents to bring younger siblings to a conference or of family members to show up at a classroom event (e.g., a holiday party) uninvited. With a new interpretation of these behaviors (recognizing the importance of the family unit in this Latino immigrant population), she has gotten more relaxed about including additional family members unexpectedly. She no longer sees their appearance as intrusive but as a natural, family-oriented behavior. She notes, "As a result of *Bridging Cultures*, I've found myself making a conscious effort to be more friendly with parents by writing more letters and thank-you notes home, letting them know I wanted to learn more from them." Now Ms. Saitzyk finds herself being invited to family gatherings and attends whenever she can. She feels closer to her students and their families and is learning a lot about their lives. Other teachers have made similar shifts in their attitudes about the presence of extended family at events designed by schools to be designed for parents alone. Because of new understanding of the value of maintaining family unity, they find themselves suspending negative judgments and even welcoming the family group.

Seeking "Everyday" Interactions

Not only do teachers appreciate the value of whole-family involvement whenever possible, they recognize the value of informal interactions that may not focus at all on academic concerns. Teacher-researcher Catherine Daley cultivates any opportunity for parent-teacher interaction because of the value she sees in it. In the segment below, she talks about how even the briefest and most informal interactions contribute to better home-school relations.

SEIZING THE MOMENT

One of our school rules directs the teachers to accompany their students to the exit gate and to remain there until the parents arrive or until the gate is closed. I take this opportunity to have mini-conferences with the parents. These conversations may never even deal with the child. They may touch on the weather or any other social topic. It may even be just a simple greeting. Yet I find that these interactions foster a closer bond with the parents.

I also encourage home visits. I find them to be very positive, and the mothers are always pleased that the teacher cares enough to make the social call for the child.

— Catherine Daley

It is clear that parents want opportunities to communicate with teachers beyond the formal events sponsored by schools. Not only Ms. Daley but other *Bridging Cultures* teachers have talked about seizing these moments for building relationships. When schools make restrictive rules for parents' entry onto the school grounds (justifiable as they may seem for safety reasons), they unwittingly curtail extremely important opportunities for cultivating parents' sense of belonging and participation and for building relationships between parents and teachers.

A recent study showed a similar pattern among 18 Latina mothers who were involved in their children's schools (Diaz, 2000). Although they wanted such formal meetings as parent-teacher conferences to extend beyond elementary school (something that is not always the case), they also expressed a desire for frequent, informal contacts with teachers and other school personnel at all grade levels. They sought impromptu encounters to find out about their children's progress and behavior, attendance, participation in nonacademic events, and the like (Diaz, 2000). It is often in the few minutes preceding or following the daily school session that parents who drop off or pick up their children have a chance to chat with teachers. In the study mentioned above, it was observed that mothers who routinely dropped off and picked up their children tended to have more consistent interaction with their children's teachers. Said one, "I pick my daughters up from school every day. There is always something about which to ask the teacher. Always, always. I am at the school all the time" (Diaz, 2000, p. 127).

UNDERSTANDING PARENTS' POINTS OF VIEW

In another example from the teacher-researchers, a potential cultural conflict arose when Giancarlo Mercado was planning a camping trip that would take students away from home for two nights. Separation had a much more negative meaning for the Latino immigrant parents than it did for parents from some of the other ethnic groups. Because Mercado talked at length with parents and understood what the field trip meant to them, a conflict was averted. In the accompanying box, he presents his account of the parent-teacher communication process he put into place — a process that ultimately resolved the problem.

THE CAMPING TRIP

For the second year the fifth grade classes are taking a camping trip away from the school site for five days and four nights. Although I teach primarily fourth grade, I also teach social studies to fifth-graders; and this year it was my job to send a letter home to parents of these students to get permission for them to go on the trip.

While the African-American and immigrant European parents quickly signed their children up, I found that I had to talk with some immigrant Latino parents individually to get them to respond. In the process of these telephone calls, I discovered that there were two major issues.

First, parents were not comfortable with having their children away from them overnight for the first time, especially without the ability to make contact with them (something that was prohibited). A few requested that we take a cell phone along, but most school staff feel that part of the value of the trip is for students to be in a natural setting without benefit of modern technology.

Second, some parents said that they would have to discuss as a family whether the child could go and how to apportion his or her responsibilities to other members of the family while he or she was gone. Here was a real example of the collectivistic values of helping and safeguarding the needs of the group over those of the individual. In this case, the potential conflict was resolved through extended discussion with parents and allowing enough time for families to work through a decision-making process that made sense to them.

— Giancarlo Mercado

Later, Mr. Mercado reflected on the issues illustrated by parents' responses to the camping trip. He noted that in his interactions with *all* parents as students left on the trip, he detected concerns for their children's safety. The difference was that some parents seemed to suppress their concerns in order to support their child's developing *independence*, but others expressed them more freely because their focus was more on the *interdependence* of the child with the family.

EVALUATING THE MESSAGES THAT SCHOOLS SEND

Bridging Cultures teachers have bemoaned the fact that although parents exhibit a great desire to be in the schools when their children are in the early grades, their interest seems to abate dramatically by the end of elementary school. There are probably several primary reasons that this happens. First, schools offer fewer formal events for parents in the upper grades (see, e.g., Diaz, 2000). Second, teachers may believe that parents have less of a role to play as academic coaches as subject matter becomes more difficult. Finally, teachers of middle and high school students (who now have many classes of students) may believe that dealing with 100 or more parents is impossible. But the falling-off of parent involvement may also be unconsciously promoted by hostile, ambivalent, or ambiguous messages communicated from school to home — despite a school's explicit policy of promoting parent involvement. In the accompanying box, the *Bridging Cultures* teacher quoted above reflects on the problem.

UNCONSCIOUSLY DISCOURAGING PARENT INVOLVEMENT

Our kindergarten classes are inundated with parents before, during, and after school. There is so much involvement that I have heard on a few occasions, "I would like to get rid of some of these parents." In these cases, teachers are making the judgment that they do not want this kind of involvement. By the time the child ends up in the fifth grade, we almost literally have to drag parents to get them into our classrooms.

What is happening between K and fifth grade? What are the messages parents are receiving in regards to being welcomed at school that filter most of them out?

— Giancarlo Mercado

As the school breakfast program problem discussed in Chapter 1 illustrates, schools need to examine the messages they are communicating to families. It is clear that messages often discourage the type of participation Latino immigrant families desire and are able to provide. Yet, despite these negative messages from the school, families are expected to participate in ways they feel less comfortable with. When they don't, sometimes unflattering and unfair judgments are made about their motivation. At the same time, schools seem unprepared to make accommodations for social and cultural differences — which, it seems, are all too often interpreted as *deficiencies* (Casanova, 1996).

BEING MORE CONSCIOUS OF THE MESSAGES SENT

As a result of analyzing the school breakfast problem in the *Bridging Cultures* training, one of the teacher-researchers (Catherine Daley) prevented the same parent blow-up in her own school. In conjunction with the establishment of a federal breakfast program in her school, the school was instructed to post signs saying, "Only students allowed in the eating area." Fortunately, Ms. Daley alerted her colleagues about the potential for misunderstanding in the community. First, she communicated this analysis to other teachers in a *Bridging Cultures* workshop she presented at her own school. At that point, disaster was averted. The bilingual coordinator intervened by writing a letter to parents explaining the district policy and assuring the parents that the decision was meant to protect the children's access to free breakfast. The coordinator also expressed the school's desire to involve them in other areas and asked for their support. She saw to it that new, friendlier signs with children's drawings on them were made and posted. Although the school was working under the same Federal guidelines as the other school (breakfast as an individual not a family entitlement) and had the same policy of excluding parents as the school in Chapter 1, the communication from school to parents was entirely different. And this made a huge difference in parent reactions: No parent objections were registered.

This example shows how the value system of individualism is built into schools (and other institutions) at the level of policy and law. The federal guidelines assumed and enforced a concept of each school child as an independent individual. The concept of the child as a member of a family unit became a violation of federal policy. Our view is that critical examination of such policies could result in regulations that would strengthen rather than undermine the family unity that immigrants bring with them but which we all need. In essence, immigrants are bringing something into society that has been disappearing, as the individualistic ethos in the U.S. becomes stronger and stronger over time. We need to recognize this collectivistic emphasis as something that fulfills a great need in our society, not something to be stamped out.

DEVELOPING CLOSER PERSONAL RELATIONSHIPS WITH FAMILIES

Bridging Cultures teachers have noticed that they are more comfortable approaching parents and responding to parents as a result of their involvement with the project. Ms. Saitzyk (the first grade teacher who found herself participating in more family events with her students) saw improvements not just in relationships but in students' achievement in her second year as part of the *Project*. She believes that the two outcomes are closely related. Her account is presented in the box below.

A TEAM EMERGES

Last year, with the class size reduction,* I had the opportunity to engage with the parents of my students more easily. I also began a reading program that required parents to participate with their children. At the same time, the *Bridging Cultures* group started. Although I had a basic connection with the culture of my students in that I majored in Spanish and I too come from a family of immigrants, it was the *Bridging Cultures* focus that made me aware of where and how I was holding back and holding on to my views, even without wanting to. It was this awareness and willingness to open to another view that made last year my most successful school year academically and interpersonally (parent involvement-wise).

   Last year I feel the parents, students, and I were a real team. The reading program required that the parent read with the child each night and return a slip noting how much time they read. There was 100% participation. Not only that, but the test scores from our May testing were excellent. My students, tested in Spanish, as a class scored way above average on overall reading. Their mathematics scores were equally high. The two English speaking first-grade classes' group scores on comparable subtests were significantly below average, markedly lower than those of my Spanish readers.

                                                    — Pearl Saitzyk

*In California, additional funds were allocated by the Legislature, beginning in the 1996-97 school year, to reduce the class size in the primary grades.

Like Ms. Saitzyk, Mrs. Pérez has consciously reached out to parents more personally and more frequently. She says, "I make more phone calls and send more notes to stay connected to parents and family. I want to keep helping children improve more. Before I only made calls when it was a problem.... Now I call to congratulate them when their student gets 'student of the month,' or when the child is really improving — when they do something wonderful as well as when there is a problem. But I make a lot more positive phone calls now. I would say I make about five calls a week... It is a very big difference." It is no surprise that parents are delighted and respond very cordially to these calls. Consequently, when Mrs. Pérez does have to call a parent about a problem she is likely to start from a basis of positive mutual regard. The fact that she discusses the child's success in terms of what it contributes to the class as a whole makes the praise culturally appropriate. The ways that teachers extend themselves personally are not "rocket science," so to speak, but cumulatively they are extremely important in developing genuine and meaningful relationships with parents.

EXTENDING OPPORTUNITIES FOR PARENT-TEACHER INTERACTION

Monthly Meetings

Conferences or other forms of parent-teacher get-togethers can be scheduled throughout the year, not just at conference time. Ms. Daley, who has taught fourth grade in partnership with another teacher, holds parent-teacher meetings about once a month "so as to keep the parents as team members and more a part of their child's development at school." She says that this process allows her to understand parents' needs and to explain hers so that they can come together in "cooperative action." She describes her efforts to build bridges to parents in the following box.

FIRST WEDNESDAYS

My team partner and I have been holding monthly parent meetings since July, 1997. The meetings are held on the first Wednesday of every month, right after school and then again at 5:30. The contents covered in these meetings vary from general announcements to going over the material in that month's unit of study.

As my school is on a year-round schedule, we found that the meeting held right before Winter vacation was particularly helpful because it allowed us to explain the homework package to parents. In that way, we could involve them in the child's work over the two-month break. It also allowed us to get a better handle on the parents' sense of being able to help their children. We found ourselves with some parents who needed further explanation on the package. A group of mothers came back the next morning asking about specific work. This made my partner and me very happy because we could see that they had reviewed the work the night before and felt comfortable enough to discuss their needs with us.

Now, these meetings didn't start out with 100% participation. In fact, out of our 38 students, only six to seven parents attended the first two meetings. The numbers have slowly improved, and most of the parents usually stay after the meetings to talk about their children or simply to chat. We've gotten to feel comfortable and supportive of each other. My Open House and parent-teacher conferences are attended by *all* of the parents. I think this has a great deal to do with the monthly meetings. While I've always wanted to hold these meetings, I don't think I'd have seen the full value in them had it not been for the *Bridging Cultures Project*.

— Catherine Daley

Comments Ms. Daley, "The way that we conduct the meetings has changed drastically [over the course of my involvement with the *Bridging Cultures Project*]. I work very hard at making sure that the parents don't see me as someone who is going to instruct them, but as someone who wants to share and ask for their input on how the children are learning."

Encouraging Parent Volunteers

Volunteering in the classroom is one form of parent involvement encouraged by most schools. But an often unspoken deterrent to a volunteer program that brings many parents into the classroom is teachers' fears that parents will not understand their instructional strategies and may be critical of them. Teachers may also worry that they do not have the time or skills to educate parents about how to participate in helpful ways. Immigrant parents may worry about not having the necessary skills to help out in the classroom. In Mexico, for example, poor people (who constitute most of the Mexican immigrants to the U.S.) usually have a maximum of six years of elementary school available to them.

Elvia Hernandez, who teaches a mixed-age lower elementary class with Kindergarten, first and second graders (K-1-2), decided to use what she was learning through the project to increase participation in her parent volunteer program. She saw a transformation in that program in the 1998-99 school year. She describes this transformation in the box below.

FROM ONE VOLUNTEER TO TWELVE

Actually, at the beginning, I had only one parent who was volunteering on a regular basis in my classroom. Because I have a multi-age classroom, I have seven families this year who were with me last year, and I thought some of those parents might feel comfortable in the classroom. Incidentally, because of the multi-age arrangement, there are some siblings placed together in the classroom. This situation allows for siblings to help each other and, on occasion, to play together — a valued opportunity from a collectivistic perspective.

In the past I would have felt intimidated to have a parent in my class while I was teaching. I thought the whole burden of teaching was mine. I would stay long hours after school doing what I needed to do to get my kids ahead. But my needs, combined with new understandings, led to new steps this year.

At our *Bridging Cultures* meetings we discussed how valuable education…is to immigrant Latino parents and how they want to continue having a role in their children's lives, including while they are at school. Keeping this in mind, and seeing the need I had, I proceeded to meet with my parents and asked them at what times they could come and what days as well. However, it took a lot more than just asking parents to give me a schedule to get them involved.

Both the parents and I had difficulty approaching each other for help. Most parents had little formal education and probably did not know how they could actually assist in the classroom; only a few had attended junior high or high school. I had to conduct my own informal ethnographic research about my families and began to build relationships with parents in the process.

Through simple conversations I had with some of them after school, I became aware of how much formal schooling they had. This gave me a good idea as to who could help my students to practice reading skills and who would rather assist putting materials together in the classroom or at home. As I became more familiar with my parents, I built a bridge between school culture, their culture, as well as my own. I started getting a better response regarding my call for volunteers.

In September, one parent (a high school graduate) was volunteering to help students during independent reading time. Soon other parents, who had accompanied their children to school, were staying on long after attendance had been taken. Sometimes they'd spend some time talking about commonalities in their homes, but I soon noticed they were talking about educational concerns. All the first-grade parents wanted their children to be reading by December. They saw how motivated the students were to read if someone read one-on-one with them even for just ten minutes. I was very excited at this point.

Although I was now averaging five parent volunteers a week, I still felt like there was something missing. Many parents would stay but were uncomfortable [interrupting me] while I was teaching a lesson and ask what they could do. They would sometimes see work they could do quickly, and then they would just sit and wait until reading time came. During my conferencing in November, I showed my parents a folder I compiled. In this folder I included a paragraph about how much I needed them to help their children achieve different academic goals. I developed a specific schedule, including days and times. I told them they were very welcome to bring younger siblings and emphasized how being in the classroom may help them (the younger siblings) when they were actually in school later on.

I typed a page addressed to each individual parent in which I explained whom they could work with and what skills to focus on. I also included a page with other activities that weren't necessarily academic that they could all help me with. I wrote a note in the folder that there was a lot of work parents could do at home for the classroom if they couldn't come during school hours because of work or any other reason. The folder was in a very visible place titled "Volunteers," so that a parent who didn't or couldn't commit herself originally would feel welcome to pick up the folder any time she could make it.

After much thought and reflection on the ideas discussed at *Bridging Cultures* meetings, some inquiry, and simple conversation with my parents, we were able to develop a system that would allow them to play an important part in their children's education and also help me out with some of my duties. I am so happy to say that I went from one parent volunteer to 12 out of the 17 families in my room.

— Elvia Hernandez

From this example, it is evident that promoting the involvement of immigrant Latino parents in the classroom is (1) possible and (2) something that requires both effort and knowledge about parents' lives. One key was to offer explicit instructions and to provide nonacademic tasks as an option, particularly welcomed by parents with little or no formal schooling. Even parents with little formal schooling have been able to make another important contribution. When it has been necessary to hire a substitute who speaks only English, parent volunteers translate from English to Spanish for the children.

Because of her success in increasing the number of volunteers in her classroom, Mrs. Hernandez was asked by the principal of her school to do a workshop on the topic with other teachers who were interested. Seventeen of the school's 25 teachers attended and are now using Mrs. Hernandez's strategies to reach the parents of their own students. Her parent folder has now been written in English as well for parents whose primary language is English. When parents who have already been through Mrs. Hernandez's volunteer "training" move on to other classrooms, they continue to volunteer. They will say, "I volunteered with Mrs. Hernandez. Could I volunteer with you?" Mrs. Hernandez reports, "One of my volunteers is now the Community Liaison between the school and the community. I gave her a reference when she applied for the job. I can see parents' confidence developing. Some of these parents may become paraprofessionals." (Of course, the ability of a teacher to attract so many volunteers depends on many factors. Mrs. Pérez reports that because so many of her students' parents are migrant workers, volunteering is not possible for them. She welcomes grandparents and other caretakers who are available.)

While this very heartening example is about increasing parent involvement in a volunteer capacity, an important strategy used to achieve this goal was *ethnography*, a technique borrowed from anthropology. This topic is further discussed in the next chapter. Although Mrs. Hernandez is herself an immigrant from Mexico, she was educated in the U.S. and did not have direct knowledge of the circumstances and histories of her students' parents. It was necessary to gain this knowledge from them personally in order to begin to form the kind of positive relationships that emerged.

PROMOTING BICULTURAL PROFICIENCY

Like all of the *Bridging Cultures* teacher-researchers, Ms. Altchech has reflected on her own efforts to help students bridge the cultures of home and school. She feels a responsibility to help her students negotiate the individualistic school system so she tries to help parents and students see why some emphasis on individual achievement is necessary. She talks with her students and parents about what it will take for students to get to college and succeed there. One research activity that she assigns is for each one to investigate a college or university and make a report to the class about it. With a more collectivistic emphasis, she also designs "Family Homework" that may require students to read to younger siblings, measure ingredients as they cook with their parents, or do some other activity in concert with other family members. Recognizing that parents emigrated to the U.S. in order to better their lives, she tries to help students acquire the skills they will need to do so, while placing these individual skills in a family context. At the same time, she attempts to aid parents in understanding the nature of the U.S. education system and the expectations it holds for their children. She believes that if families have an explicit understanding of how the expectations of home and school may differ, they can make more informed choices about helping students navigate the process of schooling.

In Ms. Altchech's classroom, students work in cooperative learning groups and are encouraged to help each other on many occasions. She notes that when she holds parent-teacher conferences, she sometimes has a tendency to focus on the report card more than she would like because she is not fully fluent in Spanish and the report card is easily translated. However, she also relies on the assistance of a classroom aide fluent in Spanish who can translate not only what she and parents say but "translate the culture." For her, reflection about the needs of her students, framed in terms of the demands of their new culture and expectations of their old cultures, is a continuous process. Only in this way, she believes, can she support students' transition to a new culture without undermining the culture of their homes at the same time.

Questions for Reflection and Research

1. What could you do to make parents more comfortable volunteering in your classroom?
2. What are stories of success with parents that you might share with other teachers? How could you (and others) build on these successes?
3. What other opportunities do you see for informal interaction with parents — between yourself and parents or schoolwide?
4. How could you help ensure that the messages sent home from your school are culturally-sensitive?

Further Reading

Fadiman, A. (1997). *The spirit catches you and you fall down: A Hmong child, her American doctors, and the collision of two cultures.* New York: The Noonday Press.

Lewis, C. C. (1995). *Educating hearts and minds: Reflections on Japanese preschool and elementary education.* Cambridge, England: Cambridge University Press.

Sheets, R. H., & Hollins, E. R. (1999). *Racial and ethnic identity.* Mahwah, NJ: Lawrence Erlbaum Associates.

Valdés, G. (1996). *Con respeto.* New York: Teachers College Press.

chapter

Teachers as Researchers

Teacher research has been strongly supported as part of teacher education; as a form of professional development; as a way to "professionalize" teaching; and as a necessary component of school reform at local, state, and national levels. "In many of these efforts, the concept of teacher research carries with it an enlarged view of the teacher's role — as decision maker, consultant, curriculum developer, analyst, activist, school leader — as well as enhanced understandings of the contexts of educational change" (Cochran-Smith & Lytle, 1999, p. 17). In other words, teacher research has been touted as a critical element of educational improvements of all kinds. Teacher research can also fulfill the purpose of broadening the general knowledge base on teaching — beyond serving the specific settings in which it is done.

In this chapter, we hope to tantalize present and future teachers with the possibility of exploring opportunities to engage in classroom-based research. It is widely agreed that teachers need opportunities to construct their own meaning from existing research, theoretical frameworks, and information from outside experts (Sparks-Langer & Colton, 1991). Such meaning-making requires reflecting on the implications of research and theory for teachers' own contexts. In addition, teachers can make valuable contributions to the field of education by doing their own action research. It must certainly be clear by now that the *Bridging Cultures Project* would be nothing without the teachers' continuous development of knowledge and classroom innovations. They are not only applying the theoretical framework in their practice but also contributing to understanding of the power of the theory itself.

Both those who have been teaching for some time and those new to teaching (including pre-service teachers doing student teaching or internships) can benefit from developing a "researcher's disposition" vis-à-vis what goes on in the classroom. Teachers are naturally curious about what happens in their classrooms, and it is a relatively short step from that curiosity to adopting a stance as researcher. Of course, students stand to benefit as well when teachers make explicit their own hypotheses about student learning and other classroom phenomena and evaluate them on the basis of observations and evidence.

In this chapter, we describe teacher "action research" and show how the *Bridging Cultures Project* fits within a particular tradition of action research. We talk about inquiry and reflection as the twin bulwarks of action research and the forms they have taken in the project. Finally, we discuss the relationship between teacher research and professional development and reflect on how teacher action research has worked for *Bridging Cultures* participants.

ACTION RESEARCH

"The term *action research* [as used originally] captured the notion of disciplined inquiry (research) in the context of focused efforts to improve the quality of an organization and its performance (action)" (Calhoun, 1993, p. 62). The roots of action research, or classroom-based research conducted by teachers, are said to lie in the work of social psychologist Kurt Lewin. But in the educational arena, we can give a great deal of credit to John Dewey. Dewey envisioned teachers as observers who engage in inquiry and use data to make informed decisions and plan intelligent interventions (Dewey, 1933). He conceived of teachers' posing hypotheses to explain educational outcomes and testing them through action — potentially contributing to theory about teaching and learning. Teacher research directly challenges the entrenched notion that university-based researchers generate the "knowledge base" for teaching, and teachers merely apply it, as well as the prevailing views of staff development and pre-service education as transmission of knowledge from outside to inside schools (Cochran-Smith & Lytle, 1993). A view of teaching practice as *inquiry* is in direct opposition to a view of teachers as merely technically skilled to carry out the research-based practice specified by institutions of higher education. Why should teachers be expected to learn about their profession strictly by studying the findings of those who are not in schools, to the exclusion of studying their own experiences? It is ironic that "[t]hose who have daily access, extensive expertise, and a clear stake in improving classroom practice have no formal ways for their knowledge of classroom teaching and learning to become part of the literature on teaching" (Cochran-Smith & Lytle, 1993, p. 5).

Unfortunately, education and other professions are still dogged by a historically established hierarchy that places basic science at the pinnacle, applied science somewhat lower, and service delivery (based on "skills") at the bottom. We know that this hierarchy belies the complexity of teachers' professional and intellectual lives — their decision-making and the (often tacit) theoretical stances that motivate their actions. Addressing classroom needs and solving classroom problems requires much more than technical skill. It requires the ability to synthesize understandings of many kinds to make decisions about instruction and about managing the interpersonal world of the classroom. Teachers need knowledge of content, pedagogy appropriate to different content domains, curriculum, learners and their characteristics, and how different approaches are linked to different philosophies of education (Shulman, 1987).

The line between professional knowledge and theory may be an artificial one. As Pagano said, "To act is to theorize" (1991, p. 194). Theory and action need to be evaluated in terms of each other (Pagano, 1991), yet teachers are not routinely invited to examine theory in light of their experiences and contribute to new ways of understanding theory. This false hierarchy of knowledge is also destructive to the whole enterprise of teaching because it results in overlooking a vast source of important knowledge about teaching. When knowledge generation is left to university-based researchers alone, the quality and usefulness of educational research are diminished (Florio-Ruane, 1991). Practitioners should be directly involved in interpreting their own practice because they have insights unavailable to staff researchers (Dinkelman, 1997). In a way, teacher-researchers' findings become a middle ground between research and practice — turning practice into research and research into practice (Kalnin, Freedman, & Simons, 1999). For these reasons, teachers ought to be active contributors to the knowledge base about teaching.

Teachers' inquiry can be directed toward several different kinds of goals. It may be focused on solving immediate instructional, learning, or behavioral problems; or it may have a broader social purpose, such as discovering how to restructure schools and teach to improve life opportunities for traditionally underserved students. The latter is associated with "critical pedagogy." This philosophical approach to teaching is grounded in ideas of social reconstruction and of reorganizing institutions so that they promote social justice for all people. It emphasizes moral and ethical concerns as opposed to technical instructional concerns. From the perspective of critical pedagogy, a teacher's ultimate goal would be to enhance equity, justice, and more humane conditions in our schools (Dinkelman, 1997; Freire, 1970; McLaren, 1989; Zeichner & Liston, 1996).

INQUIRY AND REFLECTION:
TWO INTERTWINED ELEMENTS IN ACTION RESEARCH

Inquiry and reflection are the two key components of action research. As we mentioned, despite Dewey's legacy, expectations that teachers will engage in inquiry have not always been prevalent. Nevertheless, there have been periodic efforts to promote a concept of schools as centers of inquiry (see R. J. Schaefer's 1967 book, *The Inquiring School*, for example). Perhaps there is a 30-year cycle, because current visions of schools represent "a quantum leap toward the creation of a setting where inquiry is normal and conditions of the workplace support continuous, collegial inquiry" (Joyce & Calhoun, 1995, p. 51). Inquiry implies looking beyond the immediate and seeking new information — through one's own research, through outside input from colleagues and the education community, through formal professional development, or through reading. In *collaborative* action research, the inquiry is done formally with others; but inquiry can be done less formally individually or in pairs or small groups within a school.

John Dewey and Donald Schön have shaped our ideas of what reflection is or can be. Dewey described it as behavior that involves "[a]ctive, persistent, and careful consideration of any belief or supposed form of knowledge in light of the grounds that support it and the further conclusions to which it tends" (Dewey, 1933, p. 9). He thought that three attitudes were necessary to reflection: open-mindedness, responsibility, and whole-heartedness. Without going into another layer of definitions, from Dewey's choice of elements we can almost envision the kind of teacher who is capable of a reflective stance. For reflection to yield insights, teachers have to be willing to invest part of themselves in it intellectually and emotionally, and they need to be open to self-critical conclusions. Reflection is not simply a looking back and taking stock: It incorporates thoughts about the past and present, along with plans for the future (Killion & Todnem, 1991). Ideally, reflection leads to successful changes and is not simply a philosophical endeavor. In fact, we would argue that to be worthwhile, reflection must lead to actions that have a positive effect in the classroom. Reflection is a basic ingredient in culturally sensitive teaching. "Many teachers who are effective in culturally diverse settings have learned to reflect on and grow from their own practice. These teachers have learned to examine the context in which they teach and to connect the content they teach and the learning experiences they provide with their students' daily lives and their cultural values, practices, and perceptions" (Hollins, 1996. p. 57).

Reflective practice is contrasted with technical practice (Schön, 1983; Zeichner & Liston, 1996). Reflective teachers do not simply carry out technical solutions to problems; they seek their own solutions, often with the aid of professional development or collegial learning. One implication of the reflective approach is that the solutions are not external and ready-made, nor do they entail "fixing" the student or the parent. They *may* entail changing one's own attitudes, beliefs, or actions. As Schön has observed, figuring out what the problems are and how to frame them is a serious challenge for educators. With all of our emphasis on problem-solving in education, we may "ignore problem setting, the process by which we define the decision to be made, the ends to be achieved, the means which may be chosen. In real-world practice, problems do not present themselves to the practitioner as givens. They must be constructed from the materials of problematic situations which are puzzling, troubling, and uncertain" (Schön, 1983, p. 40).

In this process of problem-setting, we identify what we think the problem is; but it could equally well be identified as something else — in light of new information or a different point of view. Without knowledge of students' cultures, even the most caring teachers may interpret behaviors based on cultural differences as developmental deficits. For instance, a student's reticence in group discussions may be interpreted as lack of knowledge, language ability, or motivation. With new cultural information, the same reticence may be seen as respectful behavior or modesty. This is an example that shows the value of outside information or evidence to the process of reflection. Reflection that is uninformed by grounds to support a conclusion (cf., Dewey, above) is an empty exercise and could even have destructive consequences.

Lack of expected performance from a student may be framed variously as a student ability problem or as an instructional problem; as a result of impoverished student experience or as a result of culturally unfamiliar curriculum content or inconsiderate instruction. How one construes low student achievement among students from nondominant cultures is not unrelated to one's views of the role of culture in teaching and learning. As Hollins (1996) explains, some teachers take a "universalistic" approach to teaching. They do not believe in taking individual or group differences into account or using different methods on the basis of cultural or other differences. Such teachers tend to locate the cause of discrepancies in performance in their students rather than in the interactions between the beliefs and practices of the dominant culture (represented in school) and those of students' home cultures. From our perspective, problem-setting based on a universalistic approach is flawed and leads to invalid solutions.

With an ongoing process of inquiry and reflection, incorporating opportunities to learn from others, teachers open to learning about their students' cultures may come to frame the problems more intelligently and thus be able to identify better solutions to them. Our *Bridging Cultures Project* provided frequent built-in opportunities for supporting inquiry, from the initial workshops and readings to the continuing group meetings where teacher researchers and staff researchers shared experiences, questions, and reflections.

TEACHERS AS RESEARCHERS
IN THE *BRIDGING CULTURES PROJECT*

Teachers have had multiple roles in the *Bridging Cultures Project* beyond that of classroom teacher: as *students* (taught by the staff researchers), as *subjects* (interviewed and observed by the staff researchers), as *researchers* (observing, taking notes, debriefing, and reflecting on their practice), and as *professional developers* (co-designing workshops, materials, and conference presentations). Of course, their primary role is that of classroom teacher, a complex role in itself. In addition to planning and carrying out instruction and assessment, they may serve on committees that require many after-school hours. Most teach courses and offer in-service workshops to their colleagues; and four are mentor teachers, who give ongoing pedagogical support to their peers.

All seven teachers have been accustomed to doing their own formal or informal classroom-based research, whether in the form of what has been called "kid-watching" (Goodman, 1985) or of gathering and analyzing formal performance data on students in order to make instructional decisions. As members of the *Bridging Cultures Project*, they have been asked to observe themselves, their students, and their students' families in new ways — to conduct inquiry on the basis of a new theoretical framework.

The term "teacher-as-researcher" often implies that the teachers themselves pose questions they want to have answered and then go about gathering data or engaging in experimentation to answer those questions. In this case, a group of staff researchers posed the broad question, "Can understanding the framework of individualism and collectivism help teachers teach their students from nondominant cultures in new and more successful ways?" At the same time, the teachers had all posed for themselves (in one way or another) the question, "How can I teach my students from nondominant cultures more successfully?" So questions generated from "inside" researchers (teachers) and "outside" researchers converged.

COLLABORATIVE ACTION RESEARCH

The tradition of teachers-as-researchers with which *Bridging Cultures* is most closely allied is *collaborative action research* (Calhoun, 1993; Sagor, 1991). According to this paradigm, a group of teachers from one or more schools works with a university partner or other education agency to define a problem and explore a set of possibilities for addressing it. Each participating institution or group contributes special expertise, for mutual benefit. In some sense, when classroom teachers and staff researchers collaborate, there are two other communities implicitly drawn into the mix: the classroom of students and the wider community of researchers and writers who have contributed to the literature read by the participants (Donoahue, Van Tassell, & Patterson, 1996).

Just to remind our readers: *Bridging Cultures* is a collaborative effort among researchers from a research-oriented university (UCLA), a teacher education institution (California State University, Northridge), a regional education laboratory funded by the federal Department of Education (WestEd), and seven teachers from three school districts. *Bridging Cultures* is not a "pure" teacher research project: It has features of both *research on teaching* (generated and conducted by staff researchers) and *teacher research* (generated and conducted primarily by teachers) (see Cochran-Smith & Lytle, 1993, for an analysis of the differences between these two forms of research). Questions that emerged from university-based research in the fields of psychology, anthropology, and education happened to intersect with the questions teachers in multicultural schools were posing. An existing theoretical framework (individualism and collectivism) previously unknown to them was the springboard for getting at teachers' understanding of their own practice and stimulating changes in it, which were documented by both teachers and staff researchers. The interpretations of events, innovations, and outcomes of the project are framed through both teacher-researchers' and staff researchers' perspectives. For example, in keeping with traditional roles, the staff researchers (the authors) have done most (but not all) of the writing about the project. However, teachers' interpretations are prominent in all of our publications, either as whole narratives, quotations, or suggested editorial changes. They read and critique everything that is written for publication. Most important, the teachers create the new educational applications of the *Bridging Cultures* framework; these applications then become self-generated findings in research on the effects of the *Bridging Cultures* training.

This kind of collaboration between teacher-researchers and staff researchers yields many benefits: access to different types of resources (intellectual, material, political); sharing of different perspectives, experience, and skills (including enhanced research skills for teachers and enhanced understanding of classroom processes for researchers); and synergistic learning based on the variety and richness of input of all participants. It offers an opportunity for teachers to make their own tacit knowledge explicit, share their insights and observations, and benefit from the constructive criticism of colleagues and others. It also brings with it several challenges: establishing a common purpose; ensuring that all participants share equally in the "profits" or positive outcomes of the collaboration; and minimizing the unconscious perpetuation of status differences that can demoralize and diminish participation.

Although collaboration may look different from project to project, it is distinguished by four characteristics :

"1. Researchers and school practitioners work together on all phases
   of the effort.
"2. The collaborative effort is focused on 'real world' as well as theoretical
   problems.
"3. Both groups gain in understanding and mutual respect.
"4. The effort is concerned with both research and development/implementation issues throughout" (Calfee, Whittaker, Wolf, & Wong, 1989, p. 3).

The Research Cycle

Collaborative action research entails an extended cycle of inquiry and reflection. Dinkelman describes a "spiraling, recursive series of at least these four steps — plan, act, observe, and reflect" (Dinkelman 1997, p. 251). As in *Bridging Cultures*, the first actual step in answering an important question may be to expand one's own knowledge by learning about existing theory and research. Data gathered through collaborative action research may be quantitative and/or qualitative. *Bridging Cultures* teachers, for example, began with open-ended inquiry focused on qualitative data. Their point of entry to the cycle mentioned above was actually "observe." They used the framework of individualism and collectivism to guide them in observing in their classrooms. They paid attention to student-student interactions, parent involvement patterns, sources of conflict between home and school, and student responses to instruction. Later they included quantitative data as well, such as before and after comparisons in numbers of parent volunteers; parent and student attendance at school events; numbers of parents requesting group versus individual conferences; and reading and mathematics scores before and after the increased parent involvement.

The data have been gathered for the following purposes: (1) to test the applicability of the theory to understanding daily life in the classroom and school community, (2) to examine implications of the theory for improving instruction and home-school relationships, (3) to document the type and frequency of innovations and evaluate their impact, and (4) to document examples of successful changes in cross-cultural instruction[1]. As the reader will have already seen, teachers have adopted many new strategies, based on their understanding of the implications of the framework. They continuously observe, ask questions, and reflect with their *Bridging Cultures* colleagues. They also plan how to act on new strategies they learn from each other, so the cycle is recursive, as Dinkelman describes it.

Tools for Collaboration

An essential component of our methodology for achieving understanding across role types of teacher-researcher and staff researcher has been dialogue. Conversations at our semi-monthly meetings allowed us to learn about each other's thinking, ways of working, and requirements for professional growth and success. It was not simply through the direct work of gathering and analyzing observational data and planning publications and presentations that we related to each other. Informal time at our meetings (often over lunch or breakfast) that was not scheduled for discussion of particular topics also allowed for dialogue between individuals or within small groups.

We have used other "discourse tools" to communicate about our learning over a period of more than three years: formal discussions on particular topics, written minutes of each meeting, e-mail messages, telephone calls, faxes, and notes from interviews and observations. Special meetings to plan presentations have been scheduled periodically. When a presentation is "ready," the presenters do a dry-run with the whole group. That way everyone has input, and the presentation is a polished piece of work that communicates effectively to its audience.

Inquiry and Reflection in *Bridging Cultures*

In the *Bridging Cultures Project*, our emphasis is not on acquisition of particular skills but on development of a thoughtful and informed approach to cultural differences in the classroom. The essence of using this paradigm is thinking and reflecting (guided by the framework) rather than providing a compendium of prescriptive interventions, although teachers have documented and shared their innovations,

---

[1] Examples of numerous instructional strategies are included in Trumbull, Rothstein-Fisch, & Greenfield, 2000.

in effect creating a compendium of practices. The project is not only collaborative across institutional lines but also collegial. That is, participants have strong inter-personal relationships and many opportunities to talk and reflect on professional concerns and support each other. Teachers and researchers critique each other's ideas and craft modified activities on the spot. For example, when one teacher decided on student-led conferences as a solution to communication problems with parents, a researcher questioned whether that practice would be harmonious with the collectivistic parents' view of adults, not children, as the leaders of the family. It wasn't long before that teacher was turning to small-group conferences (described in the previous chapter), which made sense culturally and were tremen-dously successful (Quiroz, Greenfield, & Altchech, 1999).

Initially, we did not teach specific methodologies for inquiry to the teachers. Rather, we asked them to use the framework to guide their own ongoing informal observations. Teachers were given attractive soft-bound journals for note-keep-ing. The journals were for their purposes alone, not to be analyzed by the other researchers. The idea was that even brief notes about an incident, lesson, or new way of thinking about something would jog memories for later discussion with the group. Reflection at meetings took the form of conversations (scaffolded by notes at times) or "quick writes" (teachers writing without editing for five minutes). We often saw how "[g]iven a safe place to air their uncertainties, teachers love to talk together, to share practice, and to wonder out loud about what to do with many of the real issues they face in their everyday teaching lives" (Hobson, 1996, p. 95). At the end of the initial three workshops in the fall of 1996, teachers unanimously chose to continue meeting. As we continued our sessions, we introduced the more formal notion of teachers' conducting ethnography, that is, consciously talking with parents (and sometimes students and other community members) about their background. This is discussed later in the chapter.

Bridging Cultures teachers showed evidence of reflection-*in*-action, reflec-tion-*on*-action, and reflection-*for*-action (Schön's terms). *Reflection-in-action*: Teachers reported moments when they were in the middle of instruction or inter-acting with a parent, and they had an insight into what was really happening. For example, during an open house, Mrs. Pérez had a couple of parents who got very emotional talking about the lack of education in their own lives and their hopes for better opportunities for their children. Her first inclination was to deflect the emo-tion and focus on classroom matters, but she decided in mid-stream to allow more time for acknowledging parents' personal feelings and then gently move the con-versation in another direction. She said other parents responded with empathy, saying, "That is the same with me." Her reflection-in-action was supported by what she had learned during discussions at *Bridging Cultures* meetings. *Reflec-*

tion-on-action is also common in *Bridging Cultures* classrooms. Teachers routinely employ the individualism / collectivism framework to organize reflection on events that happened in the classroom or in interactions with parents. When one teacher thought about how much her students liked helping each other and seemed slow to warm to their individual roles as class monitors, she decided to reevaluate the practice of having a single monitor. Why couldn't two students at a time serve as monitors? In a sense, her process of thinking incorporated *reflection-for-action*. Maybe sharing the job would make it more attractive; so she decided to try this new practice. Other teachers have since followed her lead.

Reflecting in a group or with another teacher seems to bring insights to consciousness that may otherwise lie below the surface for some time. Prior to a meeting in early 1999, the staff researchers asked the teachers to think about whether *Bridging Cultures* had affected their language arts instruction and, if so, how. In the course of group reflection at a *Bridging Cultures* meeting, the third-grade teacher (Amada Pérez) realized that she could conduct a short experiment in her classroom that might demonstrate the importance of "topic" to students' motivation to write. Pérez had already observed that her students produced much more writing when asked to write about "a family experience" than about "friendship." The latter had been one of the topics for the district-wide writing assessment and hadn't elicited much extended writing. She knew that anything about family — as the content of rug discussions, the topic of library books, or the subject of research projects — drew great interest from her students. But she realized that a more controlled experiment, with the wording of prompts parallel except for the actual topic, would be more persuasive in the district than her own less formal observations. "I don't know why I didn't think of doing this before!" she exclaimed.

What Pérez did was a portion of the experiment. She simulated the conditions of the district-wide assessment by designing a writing prompt that paralleled the structure of the original prompt and administering it in the same time block, without opportunities for editing or discussion. The original prompt said, "Write about a friend you have and what friendship means to you. Be sure to include who, what, where, when, why, and how." The new prompt said, "Write about an experience you had with your family. Be sure to include who, what, where, when, why, and how." She then shared the resulting essays at a faculty meeting, where everyone agreed that the length and quality of the essays on family were much greater than those on "friendship." Now the district is using the "family" prompt instead.

Critical Reflection

Bridging Cultures teachers engage in what has been called "critical reflection" (Sparks-Langer & Colton, 1991). That is, they consider how their instruction and ways of working with parents may empower students to be future citizens who are able to read critically, analyze issues, and advocate for outcomes that are in their own best interests and the interests of their communities. They recognize that this educational process is not simple and is fraught with potential culture-based conflict. They are concerned about the role of schools and schooling in a democratic society. Mrs. Pérez has actively embraced a critical pedagogical approach for many years and written about her implementation of it (1995). She has consciously used her learning about culture through *Bridging Cultures* to promote norms of communication and shared work that she believes empower her students to be critical thinkers and confident decision-makers. Although other *Bridging Cultures* teachers may not use the terminology of critical pedagogy, their actions and reflections show a critical perspective. They express the desire to see equal life opportunities for their students (e.g., to go to college, to work at jobs of their choosing) and want to support families in active construction of a school environment and educational process that promote student success. At the same time, they are not naïve about how dramatically society would have to change for their immigrant students (and their students' families) to experience true social and political empowerment.

Teachers are concerned about the social and political consequences of their teaching (Freire, 1970; Zeichner & Liston, 1996). They may be compared to Hollins's "Type III" teachers who "are likely to engage in critical analysis of the relationship among approaches to classroom instruction, students' social and cultural backgrounds, and prior school learning. They identify or develop instructional approaches that build on and extend what students learn outside of school in their homes and communities. Within the classroom, students learn from and with each other. This means that Type III teachers encourage and facilitate collaboration among students" (Hollins, 1996, p. 9). The *Bridging Cultures* teachers all teach students who, because of their collectivistic socialization, want to help each other in the classroom. Because of the *Bridging Cultures* training, mutual help among students is permitted in these classrooms and is not treated as cheating (Correa-Chavez, 1999).

Sometimes teachers with a strong social and political consciousness are moved through their own personal reflection processes to take on research projects that shake up the *status quo*. An elementary teacher (not a part of *Bridging Cultures*) documented the effects on teachers and students of a new California law barring educational and social services to "illegal immigrants." Her project resulted in a powerful, (although controversial) prize-winning documentary. Her interviews with teachers and students showed how divisive the new law was for the teaching staff and how frightening for young children who could not fully evaluate what it might mean for themselves and their families.

Some question whether the film was, in fact, a courageous and laudable effort. The "star" of the documentary, a young girl who talked candidly about her fears, may have been a casualty of the film. She and her family apparently disappeared from the school community during the course of filming, perhaps for fear of the attention the film might draw to them. The film could be criticized as actually replicating the *status quo*. One interpretation of what happened is that a teacher with higher status "set up" her colleagues and an illegal immigrant family and, in her zeal to present her own views, sacrificed the future of her own student and the safety and future of the student's family. There were repercussions for the two teachers depicted in the film as anti-immigrant (who were the ones, in a sense, set up). Both found it too difficult to stay at the school and subsequently quit their jobs. Here is an illustration of the need to consider all the possible human consequences of undertaking a social action research project. The filmmaker almost certainly did not intend some of the consequences that ensued from her project.

There are many ways to spark reflection beyond the methods we have used in *Bridging Cultures*. These may involve use of relevant popular literature and media. For example, a teacher education program at Portland State University in Oregon uses literature and movies as a spur to reflection. Teachers read books like *The Call of Stories: Teaching and the Moral Imagination* (Coles, 1989) and Tracy Kidder's *Among Schoolchildren* (1989) and watch movies like *Dead Poets' Society* (1989) and *Stand and Deliver* (1991). Small groups of teachers can initiate their own reflection groups with or without the assistance of staff researchers or professional developers. "Organizing for Diversity," a teacher professional development project based in Austin, Texas has taken the same approach (Garcia, Guerra, & Alsobrook, 2000). That project has used segments of the movies *Soul Food* (1997), *Mi Familia* (1995), and *The Joy Luck Club* (1993) to get participants talking about cultural experiences and values.

ETHNOGRAPHIC INQUIRY

As mentioned, one research method we did explore explicitly with teachers is *ethnography* (Fetterman, 1988, is a very readable introduction to it). Ethnography is "the art and science of describing a group or culture" (Fetterman, 1988, p. 11). In order to build a bridge between the culture of the school and the culture of families, especially immigrant families, the teacher must try to understand her culture and the home culture of the students. In other words, in a way, the teacher needs to become an ethnographer — a participant-observer in her classroom and in the community. Ethnography is a research method used by anthropologists to learn about cultures, usually in association with a formal research project. But any teacher who is attempting to learn about students' cultures directly from students, parents, and other community members is already engaging in informal ethnography. Ethnography may involve talking and interacting personally with children and parents and, ideally, participating in some community-based events with them. At the same time, the teacher consciously observes and takes mental notes on what she is learning. She may find out background information that allows her to make parents feel comfortable in the school environment and enables her to understand what kind of role in their children's education the parents want to and can take. An assumption underlying ethnography is that to be understood the individual must be viewed "not in isolation, but as part of an intricate web of social relationships" (Zaharlick, 1992, p. 117).

The ethnographer attempts to avoid making value judgments about what he or she observes within a cultural group (Fetterman, 1988). The risk is in judging the behaviors of one group on the basis of the values of another group (the group the observer is a member of) (Zaharlick, 1992). But most important to the value of teacher ethnography in education is a willingness and motivation to understand things from another's point of view — a motivation to empathize with a different cultural group. When one is able to see from another's point of view, the resulting empathy can allow one to keep an open mind. *Bridging Cultures* teachers have found that they are much less judgmental about the practices and beliefs of their students' families since learning about the individualism / collectivism framework and engaging in their own ethnographic observations. They now understand the positive child development goals that motivate these families' behavior and attitudes.

The framework can orient a teacher's thinking toward some of the most important issues related to child-rearing and schooling and to where conflicts may arise. Teachers may use the framework to formulate their actual questions, and they frequently use it to interpret what they hear. Parents' own experiences and their life histories can lead to understanding of students' lives and how they intersect with the culture of the classroom. One of the most relevant areas of inquiry is the parents' own educational background, including both their level of formal education and where they attended school, given that this aspect of personal history may be quite different from what the "typical" U.S. parent has experienced.

There is a difference between ethnography as practiced by anthropologists and as practiced by educators. Anthropologists have as their goal a *full description of a culture* or aspects of a culture, from the perspective of insiders — members of the culture — as much as possible. Educators add to this goal the hope that what they learn about students' cultures can be used to *improve educational practice* (Zaharlick, 1992). The translation of cultural knowledge into good educational practice is not a direct process. Two long-term educational research projects that draw on cultural knowledge — one in Hawaii and one in Alaska — have recognized this fact in different ways. In the KEEP (Kamehameha Elementary Education Program) project in Hawaii, anthropologists worked with educators to identify classroom practices that were culturally congruent with features of Native Hawaiian culture. They did not attempt to institute practices in schools that were identical to practices in homes (Au & Kawakami, 1994). However, teachers in the KEEP program were able to incorporate features of "talk story," a discourse form prevalent in Native Hawaiian culture that is "characterized by... the cooperative production of responses by two or more children" into their reading instruction (Au & Kawakami, 1994, p. 12). Because performance in collaboration with others is more highly valued by children from this culture than individual performance, teachers could elicit more participation from children during reading lessons by allowing them to respond at the same time.

We caution that moving an activity from one context to another changes it: Its purpose and meaning are not held constant. An example from a mathematics curriculum development project among Yup'ik Eskimo communities in Alaska brings home this point (Lipka, et al., 1998). Storytelling among the Yup'ik is an important way to transmit cultural knowledge, and Yup'ik children are sensitized at an early age to listen closely to the stories their elders tell. They will eventually become storytellers themselves. So, it would seem natural to use oral storytelling in the classroom as a bridge to students' culture. There's nothing wrong with that. However, if teachers expect to tell stories and have students participate by answering questions in the midst of the telling ("What might happen next?" "Why do you think she did that?"), they will be introducing a completely new norm. Traditional stories are meant to be listened to respectfully and gradually understood as children mature and gain new interpretations through life experience (cf., the Micronesian example mentioned earlier). These examples are not meant to discourage but to admit a healthy respect for the challenges of applying what is learned from ethnography to classroom settings. Nevertheless, conversations with parents and other community members, visits to homes, and attendance at social events with families all hold the promise of reducing the ignorance that even people who live in proximity to each other often have about each other.

Using an Ethnographic Approach to Solve Classroom Problems

Hollins states that "the only legitimate reason for collecting data about the background and experiences of students is for improving classroom instruction" (1996, p. 57). We would add that a reciprocal purpose is to increase the possibility that school practices do not wantonly undermine home values and parenting. If teachers and parents can establish overlapping (if not matching) goals and become conscious of where conflicts may lie, there is a greater chance of both student success and of continued harmony at home. As *Bridging Cultures* teacher-researchers became more aware of how to take an ethnographic approach, they found themselves co-solving problems with parents. This is an important point: An ethnographic approach at least temporarily removes the teacher from a superior stance vis-à-vis the parent. He or she is learning from the parent, and that fact can lead to more mutual respect. During the 1996-97 school year, Mrs. Hernandez, who teaches the K-1-2 classroom, had a first-grade student who simply wouldn't speak in class. Here is her description of what happened:

MOTHER AND TEACHER COME TOGETHER

I had had this boy since kindergarten, and he had never spoken in class. As concerns mounted, the principal and others began to suggest he might belong in a special education class. I really believed the child had normal ability, and I decided I would have to work closely with the child's parents, if the problem were to be solved.

I talked with the mother, asking her about her own educational background and tried to feel out what might be an appropriate way for her to be involved in solving the problem. I discovered that she was literate, having moved to the United States after elementary school and finished high school and some college here. She was able to read to the child and help him with literacy skills. It was very frustrating at first, but she persisted. For my part, I treated him just like the other children. Finally, he gradually started speaking in class. After a while I could see that his math skills were really coming along, and then he started reading well.

At the end of the year, this boy scored in the 96th percentile on the standardized math test and in the 85th percentile in reading (both in Spanish). I know that if I had not had the support of the mother and we had not both held out the expectation that this child would achieve, we might have been meeting at the end of the year to discuss alternatives that neither of us would have felt good about.

— Elvia Hernandez

Mrs. Hernandez has an advantage over some other teachers, not only because she comes from the culture that many of her students come from, but also because she has most of her students for three years. Sometimes she has two or even three children from the same family, including siblings and cousins, and so she gets to know families in a special way.

Another teacher-researcher (who teaches kindergarten) told of a related experience she had. Her problem solution was based on gaining knowledge of the neighborhood conditions and of the parents' situation at home. At a more basic level, this knowledge was accompanied by an ability to identify with parents, which led to an unexpected and positive outcome.

THE ATTENDANCE PROBLEM

I was sitting in a faculty meeting with a large group of teachers one afternoon, and the topic of attendance came up. We have a chronic problem keeping our attendance rates up, and teachers were discussing whether there was anything that could really be done about it. The tone was fairly negative. Finally, I said that I thought a lot of the problem had to do with the fact that the parents often had no support at home, no one who could stay with a younger child who was sick, for example. It isn't safe for children to walk to school alone in our neighborhood, so parents' only recourse under those circumstances is to keep the child at home.

It occurred to me that parents could somehow "buddy up" and help each other get children to school when there was an emergency. Families with children live near each other, but I was hesitant to take a prescriptive approach or hand out names and addresses to the whole group without parents' involvement and agreement. What I began to do was approach parents in ones and twos and ask them how they thought we could solve the problem, and they themselves suggested they could find parents near them so that they could help each other. Some of them started walking together to see where each other live. Now I often actually see a parent walking two children to or from school. There have been many occasions when a child has been able to come to school because of this informal, parent-organized system when he or she would otherwise undoubtedly been left at home.

(see overleaf)

This may be a small example of change, but I have noticed that I am taking a new tone toward parents. When you say, "We've got a problem; we need help," versus "You need to do this" (whatever it is), they will absolutely help. In our group conferences, we talked about how we have to help each other. I will ask them with regard to a problem, "What do *you* think?" It seems to make all the difference in the world.

— Kathryn Eyler

Anthropological fieldwork is said to be "transformative in that it changes the fieldworkers themselves by increasing their understanding of how culture affects their own behavior and that of others..." (Zaharlick, 1992, p. 123). Teachers do not usually have the opportunity to engage in the lengthy fieldwork of the anthropologist, but it is evident that *Bridging Cultures* teachers' closer encounters with the communities of their students have been transformative for them as well.

Practical Suggestions for Engaging in Ethnography

Posing Diplomatic Questions

Because teachers, unlike anthropologists, may not have an opportunity to observe in their children's homes, much has to be learned through conversation with parents; often this will take place in parent-teacher conferences. In order to learn through conversation, diplomatic questions must be constructed. Diplomatic questions do not appear invasive, because they are based on background knowledge rather than ignorance; the teacher can use this knowledge to make her information-seeking more indirect (this point was elaborated upon in Chapter 3, this volume).

For example, if a teacher wants to ask an immigrant mother how far she went in school, she can first ask two nonthreatening questions: "Where are you from?" and "How old were you when you came to the United States?" As an example, the mother may answer that she is from rural Mexico and that she was educated there. The teacher can now use her knowledge of Mexican schooling to transform what could be a threatening probe into a welcoming one: "I know that some places in Mexico do not have schools available, or they exist only up to sixth grade. It must have been difficult for you to get an education in Mexico." It is important to notice that this probe is *not* in the form of a question. The statement shows relevant background knowledge, rather than ignorance, making it a socially competent conversational move, not an intrusive probe. Because it is both *indirect* and *knowledge-based*, it should meet with a positive response and successfully elicit a story about school. A parent may say, "Yes, I had only one year of school. The school was too far from our *ranchito* [little farm]." This is the kind of questioning discussed earlier in the Chapter 3 section, "Culture and Communication in the Parent-Teacher Conference." Of course, it is not fair to assume that because a parent is an immigrant, he or she has not had the opportunity to complete a course of higher education. The point is that educational opportunities in Mexico vary greatly, depending upon where one lives, and it is important for the teacher to know what the parent has had access to.

Interpreting Information

What can a teacher do with this information? Well, now she knows that this mother would have difficulty teaching her child academic skills at home. More likely, as suggested earlier, she would be interested in *learning with* her child. In a study of parent-teacher conferences, one conference involved an immigrant mother who had a first-grade education (Greenfield, Quiroz, & Raeff, unpublished data, 1995). The teacher talks with her about *teaching* her child at home; she replies that she loves to learn *with* her child. The teacher does not appear to notice this transformation by the mother and does not seem aware of the mother's educational level. Miscommunication has occurred. Had the teacher known to find out about the mother's educational level, it would not have happened. Indeed, she could have encouraged the mother to learn *with* her child. For immigrant mothers with little education, this ethnographic process could lead to alternatives to the more standard "mother as teacher" role and result in better consequences for both mother and child.

Another thing a teacher can do is ask parents for *their* interpretation of a child's behavior when the child is having a problem. The situation of the little girl and the blocks in Chapter 1 would have been a perfect opportunity for the teacher to hear another interpretation of what was going on. Had the teacher asked the mother how she saw the same scenario, she might have learned something important about a different perspective. The norm in the home may well have been to share all the toys whenever another child was around. This is not to say that the rules of the classroom must be equivalent to those of home; rather, the rules in both settings can be made explicit, so children understand what is expected of them. Incidents like these can be grist for the mill in the parent conference, if enough trust has been built to allow parent and teacher to listen to each other in good faith.

Preparing for Ethnographic Inquiry

The ethnographic process requires background knowledge. A teacher cannot expect to know how to frame questions that will elicit useful answers without having
done some homework in advance. Sources of information that teachers may find
useful are local newspapers, books on specific cultures, and pamphlets from social
service or educational agencies. The California Department of Education has a
series of short books on the culture of several ethnic groups, including Chinese,
Vietnamese, Japanese, and Hmong (1994). Teachers or other school personnel,
such as paraprofessionals who come from the students' cultures, and personal
observation` are also important sources of information. Of course, the more the
teacher can learn the better; however, the most basic understanding can go a long
way toward starting a productive conversation. Background knowledge — both
general to culture and specific to each individual — is crucial to understanding
students and their families.

The most important background information on Mexican immigrants concerns the sociology of schooling in Mexico. The vast majority of poor people
receive only elementary instruction. After the elementary level, schooling becomes
expensive and is not available in every community. Even elementary schooling is
not geographically accessible to people who live on farms out in the country. High
school not only costs money but is offered only to an elite who can pass an
entrance examination. Books, materials, and preparation for the entrance examination are also affordable only by the elite. In a sample of poor immigrant Latinos in
West Los Angeles, a typical educational pattern was a mother with some elementary school education and a father who had attended junior high (Greenfield,
Quiroz, & Raeff, 2000). Diaz (2000), in her study of 18 Latina mothers who were
actively involved in their children's schools, also found that of these women who
had emigrated from Mexico as adults most had not had more than six years of
formal schooling. If a teacher has this level of knowledge about the educational
system in Mexico, he or she can use it as a basis to ask informed questions to learn
about the actual experiences of the parents of his or her students. Of course,
individuals' experiences will vary tremendously, and that must be kept in mind.

A major reason families emigrate or migrate is to provide their children with
more education than they can get in Mexico. However, such families have relatively collectivistic ideals and do not share the more individualistic value system
that higher levels of schooling promote and require. On the whole, they do not
have as much experience with formal education as their children's teachers. On the
one hand, their collectivistic value system leads such parents to socialize their
children for "good behavior," in an approach to child development that is more
"holistic" than one that focuses on cognitive skills. In addition, the teacher's role

and greater level of formal education leads these parents to respect her authority in teaching cognitive skills (Greenfield, Raeff, & Quiroz, 1996). Bridging this disparity in values and experiences has been the major focus of this *Guide*. Of course, it should not be assumed that these generalizations alone predict the background or academic outcome of any individual; nor does any one system of values or education have unmitigatedly positive results, as we know. Rather, these observations provide some likely context for inquiry.

The Issue of Indigenous Languages

In the present wave of Mexican immigration, there are many indigenous or "Native American" people who come to the U.S. speaking an Indian language, often without knowing either Spanish or English. (An example is the Zapotec Indians in Venice, California, a large indigenous community from Mexico who settled in the Los Angeles area.) Thus, school personnel need to be aware of the possibility of indigenous "Latino" students who do not speak Spanish. An important educational question in the U.S. is whether such children should start out in Spanish-speaking classrooms or go straight to English. The issue is complicated by the fact that Indians have, since the Spanish conquest, suffered oppression and discrimination at the hands of other Mexican immigrants, who may refer to their language derisively as "dialect" (reported by Giancarlo Mercado).

Ethical Concerns

Any kind of research brings with it a set of ethical concerns. Personal information about individuals should not be shared with others without written permission, and trust between teachers and parents is built on the belief that confidentiality will be respected. Ethnography is not meant to be invasive. Teachers who are conducting ethnographic inquiry have to judge carefully how comfortable parents and students seem to be as they talk about different topics. A teacher needs to ask herself whether the questions she is asking are likely to produce information that *will* help her teach better or relate to parents better. Gratuitous probing into people's private lives is, obviously, not ethical. From an academic ethical perspective, research "must have some bearing on the development of knowledge and in some way contribute to the social good" (Fetterman, 1988, p. 122). The professional ethics of teaching dictate nothing less. Teachers are, of course, mandated reporters. They are required by law to report instances of child abuse or reasonable evidence to suggest such abuse, maltreatment, or neglect. However, when teachers learn deeply about cultures they are less likely to misinterpret local practices that on the surface may seem to point to abuse but are, in fact, benign. For example, in many cultures, children are trained and expected to care for younger children (Weisner & Gallimore, 1977). However, when this practice is brought to the U.S. it can be considered abusive rather than an example of socially responsible behavior on the part of the older child.

An Example of Ethnographic Inquiry by Teachers in the M-CLASS Project

Teacher research can take many forms. Some projects involve networks of teachers from around the country. The M-CLASS Project (Freedman, Simons, Kalnin, Casareno, & The M-CLASS Teams, 1999) is also a collaboration among university researchers and school-based researchers; but in this case the focus is on literacy instruction and learning in urban high schools that are multicultural. Teachers from the Boston area, New Orleans, Chicago, and the San Francisco Bay Area worked with researchers from the National Writing Project to explore what made for successful literacy instruction with diverse populations of students. A unifying philosophy among the group was critical pedagogy: They believed that successful schooling would be empowering to students, supportive of their development as the people they were rather than forcing them to forgo their personal identities as a condition of success. They envisioned ideal schooling as promoting social justice through student empowerment.

The groups of teachers themselves represented considerable diversity on the basis of race, ethnicity, gender, and class. They realized that if they were going to have an ongoing dialogue about multicultural education, they needed to learn about each other, "come together as 'ethnographers,' [and] open up to each other's realities..." (Simons, Daniels, Yearwood, & Walker, 1999, p. 144). An explicit goal of the teachers' research through the project was to understand how to help students achieve a multicultural literacy that draws on the literature, history, and experience of their own communities. They wanted to make their curricula more relevant to their students, something that would raise issues often skirted by schools — issues such as racism, racial history, classism, White privilege, and the like. The M-CLASS teachers believed that successful instruction required understanding of and empathy for their students. They would need to learn much more about their students' personal lives as well. In short, teachers would be using teacher research to see each other, "their students, themselves, their classrooms, or all of these in new and unexpected ways" (Freedman, with Wood, Austin, McFarland, & Potestio, 1999, p. 89). Ethnographic inquiry was thus a core component of the project.

English teacher Eileen Shakespear of Boston posed the two-pronged question, "What can we observe about the relationship between Black male students and White female teachers that can enlighten and better inform our class practice? How does the relationship affect the students' literacy learning?" (Freedman et al., 1999, p. 232). As she observed, "...education happens in relationships, so shouldn't we study those relationships?" (Shakespear, 1999, p. 78). To begin to answer questions which Shakespear acknowledged might "shed some harsh light on her own work," she used several research techniques. First, she took notes on her own practice and wrote reflections in her journal. Then she decided to interview André, a Black male student whom she perceived as exceptionally insightful. From there, she asked André to conduct interviews with five other Black male students. Finally, Shakespear interviewed two White female teachers whom she and others thought had been particularly successful with Black male students.

Shakespear found that her research yielded insights that ordinary teacher-student interactions could not. Because of these young men's experiences they held a lot of anger toward Whites. They reported being targets of police observation; being followed in stores; being in cars that were stopped, evidently, on the basis of racial profiling; being understimulated in schools by teachers who underestimated their intellect. At the same time, they didn't want to insult a teacher they perceived as caring about them. Through the interviews (audiotaped), Shakespear came to understand these boys' thoughts about race and schooling, especially how schools and teachers could be expected to "mess you up." To summarize their complex narratives would do a disservice to them, but it must be said that the ethnographic interviews taught Shakespear important things about these students she would never have learned through ordinary classroom discussion, no matter how well-managed and topically relevant to the students.

TEACHER RESEARCH AS PROFESSIONAL DEVELOPMENT

Collaborative action research can serve as a form of professional development (Burnaford, 1996; Burnaford, Fischer, & Hobson, 1996; Sagor, 1991). Professional development has been broadly defined as "Whatever enhances the lives and work of teachers" (Burnaford, 1996, p. 139). A more specific way of characterizing the purpose of professional or staff development might be, "to alter the professional practices, beliefs, and understanding of school persons toward an articulated end" (Guskey, 1986). Certainly, observation guided by clear questions and a framework for understanding what is observed can yield changes in thinking and practice. Such a process entails taking considerable responsibility for one's own learning, a degree of autonomy associated with a norm of continuous inquiry (cf., Barth, 1990; Joyce & Calhoun, 1995). This kind of professional development holds the promise of deeper learning and greater levels of application, compared to the usual in-service programs. According to Oja and Smulyan, "Teachers who participate in action research projects become more flexible in their thinking, more receptive to new ideas, and more able to solve problems as they arise" (1989, p. 15).

Too often in-service programs show teachers how to teach differently but do not provide a thorough rationale for the innovations they recommend or encourage opportunities for teachers to critique and adapt an innovation to suit their own situations (McLaughlin, 1990). Even the most well-received in-services may not be translated into altered practice for lack of adequate support in the implementation phase (Guskey, 1986; McLaughlin, 1990). And we believe that when professional development is prescriptive without offering a theoretical, research-based rationale for why it should work, it undercuts teachers' ability to interpret and innovate intelligently. Speaking in behalf of teacher inquiry, Ingvarson says, "[T]he most effective avenue for professional development is cooperative study by teachers themselves into problems and issues arising from their attempts to make their practice consistent with their educational values... [The inquiry approach to professional development] aims to give greater control over what is to count as valid educational knowledge to teachers" (1987, pp. 15, 17).

Teacher change does not proceed neatly from changes in beliefs and attitudes to improved classroom practice, to enhanced student outcomes (Guskey, 1986; McLaughlin, 1990). More often, teachers need to get into the implementation phase of an innovation and see some outcomes before their beliefs and attitudes change. In *Bridging Cultures*, teachers were exposed to new ideas, but they were given no suggested changes in practice. On their own, they began to test these new ideas and experiment in ways that made sense to them.

Good collaborative action research is likely to have many of the features of good professional development. According to Little (1993), good professional development:

1. Offers meaningful intellectual, social, and emotional engagement with ideas, materials, and colleagues
2. Takes explicit account of the contexts of teaching and the experience of teachers
3. Offers support for informed dissent
4. Places classroom practice in the larger contexts of school practice
5. Prepares teachers (as well as students and parents) to employ the techniques and perspectives of inquiry
6. Should involve governance that ensures a balance between the interests of individuals and the interests of the institution

We might add a seventh principle:

7. Addresses important concerns related to the educational success of all students, particularly that of students from nondominant cultures, who are frequently underserved by the educational system

While not all schools have ethnically or linguistically diverse populations, nearly all have groups of students whose needs tend to be ignored by standard professional development. We contend that any good professional development will consider how to improve education for these students in particular and not just so-called "mainstream" students.

Table 5.1 presents *Bridging Cultures* teachers' comments about the nature of the *Bridging Cultures* collaboration and professional development and its effects on them. These comments came as answers to specific questions from the staff researchers about their recollections of the initial three workshops (including content, process, and people involved) and their thoughts about ongoing meetings. For that reason, they do not address all of Little's principles. Nevertheless, they do give a strong sense of how the professional development, which gave way to collaboration, engaged and challenged teachers and was highly applicable to their teaching contexts.

Table 5.1
Teachers' Comments about *Bridging Cultures* Collaboration
and Professional Development

With regard to the group...

I felt a kinship with everybody there. We were all coming from the same place, even though we weren't all the same.

— Kathy Eyler

It was a great team with diverse educational backgrounds and talents. It was a great opportunity to learn from peers that had different experiences that all lead to one commonality. Good group. [It was] nice to be involved with university people for a change instead of just elementary or high school teachers... Because we are all driven by the same force, that has made our bond stronger...[W]e have an aligned vision of Bridging Cultures. We have a mutual base of support and a powerful professional network.

— Marie Altchech

It was a good group of people.... A group of people who cared very deeply about teaching and students and wanted to understand more....

— Pearl Saitzyk

With regard to the effects of the workshops and meetings...

I was overwhelmed — a tidal wave going over my head — not knowing how to filter it or sort it out... constant flashbulbs. It was in the discussion after the scenarios, talking about the individualistic and collectivistic responses and realizing that I was more of an individualistic [responder] but still saw the collectivistic point of view. That was overwhelming.

— Catherine Daley

It was like an awakening to realize that people of a different culture would see things so totally differently. It was something that I had not thought of to that extent. It was "Ah hah!" Very enlightening — the whole notion of a Euro-American person's view as a cultural point of view. And I have that.

— Pearl Saitzyk

I have been to every single meeting. I don't want to let it go. I feel strongly about continuing, because it was so mind-awakening and thought-provoking. It really distances itself from common professional development, because it wasn't a one-shot deal.... We opened a book, a box; and you have all these things in the box and [begin to find out] why some things are in the box. You have a puzzle. It is still a mystery, because you haven't known about it. The box is yourself. There is never any final, real closure to this. It is ongoing.

— Giancarlo Mercado

With regard to the process of the workshops and meetings...

It is always nice to have your professional work and opinion valued and deemed important by other colleagues. This is one of the changes of [going] from subject to collaborator. Others listen and hear what you are doing, and that is a good thing. When you are a subject, you are scrutinized because "we want to grow the project."

— Marie Altchech

I remember the professionalism with which we were treated and the professional manner with which the whole project was conducted.

> We were given a thorough explanation of the theories behind the project and the purpose of the [first] three meetings. We were also allowed and invited to state our opinions freely, even if they tended to get emotional.... I felt respected and uncensored.... I felt I was part of the team of people doing legitimate work that I could take into my classroom and could actually change my method of teaching.
>
> — Elvia Hernandez

> The best aspects of the meetings are the connections and the dialogue and the opportunity to share successes.... I've gone to lots and lots of meetings in my professional life — often going off on tangents of negativity. But in our meetings, we share successes — lots of excitement and a only little negativity, in spite of the difficult times for the state and big changes over testing...all the anti-immigrant laws and hysteria in the media. We have touched on those things, but it is in the spirit of sharing and moving on with our business. It is different from what I have seen in other places.
>
> —Amada Pérez

A recent characterization of good professional development adds features of "longer duration with more open-ended personal commitments" and "iterative co-construction of agenda by teachers and professional developer[s] over time" (Stein, Smith, & Silver, 1999, p. 244). Leadership training for the teachers is also cited as important. With these various characterizations of professional development, one gets the picture of a dynamic process that promotes mutuality rather than a one-sided transmission of knowledge.

Collaborative research provides something that may not be present in traditional professional development, particularly of the "in-service" variety: the opportunity for *ongoing* discussion, dialogue, and reflection. In *Bridging Cultures*, we have been having incredibly rich interactions around a common topic for more than four years. These interactions have supported teachers to engage in many creative actions that have enhanced their teaching practices, their classroom environments, and their communication with parents. Collaborative action research projects can serve as professional development for staff researchers as well. The same potential is there for reflection about their practice, shared critique (if status differences can be mitigated), and support for improved ways of conducting their work. It goes without saying that the focus is usually on teachers' changes and not those of the staff researchers. Nevertheless, in the course of writing this book on the *Bridging Cultures Project*, we, the staff researchers, have been forced to reflect on our practices. How might we have organized the project differently (since we had responsibility for that at the outset)? To what degree did we achieve mutuality with the teachers? Did we hear them when they emphasized that something was important? How could we do better next time? We are still attempting to answer these questions on the basis of what teachers have said and what we have observed.

HOW SUCCESSFUL HAS COLLABORATIVE ACTION RESEARCH BEEN IN THE *BRIDGING CULTURES PROJECT*?

At one time or another *Bridging Cultures* participants have experienced all of the benefits and challenges mentioned earlier in this chapter. Teachers were immediately stimulated by the university-based research and theory and eager to explore how it could be applied in their classrooms. Staff researchers were excited when these capable and invested teachers discovered applications of the theory in new situations and constructed practices that successfully implemented the theory. Teachers gloried in the opportunities to discuss their observations with their peers and reveled in their deepening understanding of the implications of individualism and collectivism, as additional research and theory were discussed in light of their classroom-based examples.

The norm of reflection and analysis that comes with the territory of being a researcher is not routinely incorporated in school culture, where teachers have little time for collegial interactions (Cuban, 1992). However, this research norm was in harmony with what the teachers wanted for themselves. In fact, they had apparently cultivated "a professional problem-solving ethos" (Calhoun, 1993, p. 62) prior to participation in the project. They had no difficulty in engaging in discussions of professional practice for hours on end over a period of years. Despite long commutes for some to our Saturday meetings, teachers always stayed later than the scheduled time to discuss their students, families, their instructional practice, school, district, or state policies affecting their students, and many other issues.

One benefit of collaborative action research for teachers should be exposure to new methods of inquiry or support to use methods with which they may not have had much experience. Ethnographic inquiry was certainly something that some teachers used informally without having invoked a formal label for it. But the project validated it and extended it to other teachers; and it became a more conscious tool for learning. The initial exposure to the framework of individualism and collectivism gave teachers additional background knowledge that in some cases enabled them to become more involved with their students' families and become better ethnographers. The stories in this chapter, as well as several others in earlier chapters, illustrate that. To suggest that teachers have adopted a clinical distance from families and are rigorously conducting research on them and their communities would be to mischaracterize their relationships. Rather, they are able to use new information to make more thoughtful inquiries and feel increased comfort with families.

Another fortunate compatibility in the project was that both staff researchers and teacher researchers have "gotten their needs met." Staff researchers have been able to satisfy their research interests (and satisfy professional and funding requirements for publications and presentations), and teacher researchers have discovered many ways to improve their instruction and relationships with students and parents (cf., Cuban, 1992; Hattrup and Bickel, 1993). Participation in the project has also supported teachers' expanded roles as professional developers themselves, and five of the seven teachers have developed considerable skill in making presentations. They have been eager to share what they have learned and have presented at numerous state and national conferences, offered workshops to their colleagues in their schools and districts, and (in the case of two teachers) incorporated *Bridging Cultures* ideas into courses they teach to teacher-interns. This process, in turn, has disseminated the *Bridging Cultures* framework to the educational community, both national and local. The mutuality of benefit that we describe is a key to a successful cross-institution collaboration, we believe. In *Bridging Cultures,* however, the whole point was to learn about how teachers' thinking and practice might change as a result of exposure to cultural theory and research — not to teach them an intervention and observe to determine whether it was faithfully implemented and what the outcomes were.

Great claims have been made for the benefits of teacher research, but they don't seem outrageous when we look at the outcomes of our project (and it's not over yet!). Among the benefits cited by Goswami and Stillman (1987, in Cochran-Smith & Lytle, 1993) are (abbreviated and paraphrased):

1. Teaching is transformed in important ways; teachers become theorists, testing their assumptions, and connecting theory to practice.
2. Teachers' perceptions of themselves as writers and teachers are transformed.
3. Teachers become more active professionally and more conscious resources to the profession.
4. Teachers become more critical users of current research, less vulnerable to the latest fad, more authoritative in their evaluation of curricula, materials, methods.

As we survey the teachers of *Bridging Cultures*, we believe all of these effects have taken place. However, we must acknowledge that from the beginning the teachers demonstrated a strong inclination to connect theory and practice and to engage in inquiry to develop their knowledge and skills. Almost certainly, the project could not have worked without these initial attitudes. Table 5.2 presents some reflective comments made by teachers about the effects of the project on their own professional roles and the ways they find themselves disseminating *Bridging Cultures* ideas. It is important to recognize that any project of this nature will have different effects on different participants. For example, not every teacher will feel comfortable making presentations to large — or even small — groups. In the *Bridging Cultures Project*, even teachers who do not want to take a formal professional development role with others are finding themselves interacting with colleagues and parents in new ways and sharing their newfound insights.

TABLE 5.2
Teachers' Comments Reflecting Impact
of *Bridging Cultures* on Their Professional Role

When I go into a meeting with the school counselor, I have the guts to say, "This is what the parents need."...Whenever I talk about certain philosophy with mentees or team members, or with people in the office about a situation, I will always use the model of *Bridging Cultures* if it is appropriate. Over 50% of the time it *is*. ... And there are times when teachers ask, "Is it cultural or developmental with children." And I think, "I really don't know." I'm still chewing on this.
— Catherine Daley

I have discussed how culture is important in the development of the child. It is especially important to me to discuss with other teachers when they express a clash between their expectations and the reality of how a child performs. It is a problem there, because they expect certain things from a child in school, and [what they get] is not exactly what they expected...[e.g.,] They expected the child to work independently with hardly any adult supervision...I spoke with a third-fourth grade teacher, and she thought that parents didn't care about how their children did in school or that they were getting behind each year, because they weren't at grade level. She basically thought it was the parents' fault. I explained it was not necessarily true. It didn't necessarily mean parents didn't care. It was dependent upon what parents valued as important, and that is what parents and kids came in with. It was a matter of explaining what she wanted to the parents, so they would understand. That really makes me upset, when I hear blanket statements, when teachers blame the parents. I stick up for parents now.... I also try to speak out to the parents and explain school policies to them.... I have become more open to speaking with parents and teachers.... I have learned to see things from the administrator's view and the other teachers' views. The principal has asked me to be a liaison between teachers unwilling to otherwise work together.

I feel more confident to face parents when problems arise, because I try to see things from their eyes before I pack on information. I have tried to help less experienced teachers deal with parents and administration.

— Elvia Hernandez

I am more effective in working with parents. There is more of a connection between school and parents in my classroom, and parents have been helping more because I have been more specific about how they can help...As part of the reading program, there was a parent component that I never did before. This was the first time I did it and got great results.

— Kathy Eyler

I had to give a presentation to Reading Recovery teachers about [how to involve] parents. So I started talking about the *Bridging Cultures* Project and the purpose of it and about individualism and collectivism — how a greater awareness is needed. I talked about how it affected me in my classroom. I spoke about my relationships to my own parents, and how it [participation in the project] led to more openness, curiosity and flexibility on my part. They had never thought of it that way...They found it very interesting.

— Pearl Saitzyk

I have introduced the framework to people at school who want to listen. They have to be ready to listen. With those people who attended a mini-in-service, they now do group parent conferences...The opportunity to present at the NAME conference with Elise [Trumbull] in St. Louis in November, 1998 was very important for me in terms of a professional development opportunity to share about the project with others.

— Marie Altchech

I am a literacy facilitator on the district literacy group. It's like a mentor position. Because of that, I am able to do informal discussion and bring our *Bridging Cultures* framework in, like using children's lived experiences in district-wide writing samples. I've contributed

ideas for the report card and parent conferences...that kind of thing.
I have also been a grade level representative and shared my ideas
in those meetings. In my school, I gave a *Bridging Cultures* presentation at a faculty meeting. And I've enjoyed being able to give workshop and conference presentations with other members of the group
in California and around the country.

— Amada Pérez

I've presented the model to colleagues, to my district, and to other
schools. I've presented in California and in other states — locally,
statewide, and nationally. On a one-to-one basis I have presented it
to all my fellow mentors and my mentees. I have infused it in my
course at UCLA, Diversification of Social Studies Curriculum, and in
presentations to district interns in the Social Science Methods class
— as well as to District Intern Program instructors.

— Giancarlo Mercado

[Note: Los Angeles Unified School District has a teacher intern program for preparing new teachers.]

A HOPE AND A TOUCH OF REALITY

We hope we have succeeded in making the case for teachers-as-researchers. We have seen how a focus on a common question can galvanize inquiry and
reflection. Collaboration with staff researchers can supply additional stimuli and
new frameworks for inquiry that build on teachers' natural problem-solving incli-
nations. We know that teachers do not always get the kind of institutional support
that is needed to make schools places of inquiry for both themselves and students. Members of another collaborative action project commented that despite
the clear need for opportunities to come to know and appreciate children's out-of-
school lives, as a group they found little institutional support for such opportunities. They say, "Making opportunities for professional reflection and collaborative growth a normal part of teachers' lives will, we know, require widespread
changes of institutional structure, professional vision, and public will" (Dyson, et
al., 1997, p.). The time may be ripe for this kind of change, though. Calls for
"professional practice schools" (Lieberman & Miller, 1990) and greater inclusion
of practicing teachers in research are widespread (see, e.g., Cochran-Smith &
Lytle, 1999).

Competing demands and needs, however, may jeopardize the future of teacher
inquiry. Current pressures for accountability at the classroom, school, and district

level seem to be resulting in increased reliance on "expert models" of reform based on outside research. As districts buy into packaged reforms that by their very nature overlook local context and "the construction of local knowledge in and by school communities, [they also]… de-emphasize the role of the teacher as decision maker and change agent" (Cochran-Smith & Lytle, 1999, p. 22). As with many other aspects of public education, responses to outside pressure through a seemingly defensible strategy may inadvertently result in the demise of other valued practices that stand to benefit institutions more. In the case of teacher research, this would be an extremely unfortunate loss.

Questions for Reflection and Research

1. What kinds of questions do you have that might be at least partially answered by action research?
2. Whom might you collaborate with to organize a research project around one or more of those questions?
3. If you are already teaching, what other resources do you have outside of your immediate school to support such action research?
4. What would be a good first step you could take for action research relevant to your setting?
5. How would you begin an ethnographic study of your students? What observations would you need to make? What questions would you ask... of whom?

Further Reading

Burnaford, G, Fischer, J., & Hobson, D. (1996). *Teachers doing research: Practical possibilities*. Mahwah, NJ: Lawrence Erlbaum Associates.

Donoahue, Z., Van Tassell, M.A., and Patterson, L. (Eds.), (1996). *Reading in the classroom: Talk, texts, and inquiry*. Newark, DE: International Reading Association.

Zeichner, K. M., & Liston, D.P. (1996). *Reflective teaching: An introduction*. Mahwah, NJ: Lawrence Erlbaum Associates.

...with an Ethnographic Focus

deMarrais, K.B. (Ed.), (1998). *Qualitative research reflections*. Mahwah, NJ: Lawrence Erlbaum Associates.

Freedman, S. W., Simons, E. R., Kalnin, J. S., Casareno, A., & The M-CLASS Teams (1999). *Inside city schools: Investigating literacy in multicultural classrooms*. New York: Teachers College Press; and Urbana, IL: National Council of Teachers of English.

Gonzalez, N., Moll, L., Floyd-Tenery, M., Rivera, A., Rendon, P., Gonzalez, R., & Amanti, C. (1993). *Teacher research on funds of knowledge: Learning from households* (Educational Practice Report No. 6). Santa Cruz, CA: National Center for Research on Cultural Diversity and Second Language Learning (now CREDE) (e-mail crede@cal.org).

Lipka, J., with Mohatt, G. V., & The Ciulistet Group (Eds.). (1998). *Transforming the culture of schools: Yup'ik Eskimo Examples*. Mahwah, NJ: Lawrence Erlbaum Associates.

Valdés, G. (1996). *Con respeto*. New York: Teachers College Press.

chapter 6

Conclusion:
The Challenge of
Coming Together

Finding common ground among parents, students, teachers, and the school as a cultural institution is obviously a task that reaches well beyond individual teachers. But common ground cannot be based on an erasure of cultural differences. It must be based on an understanding of and positive respect for fundamental differences in cultural values. Probably the most fundamental differences in cultural values are the ones we have focused on in this guide — the differences between individualism, a cluster of basic American values, and collectivism, the values of American Indians and the ancestral values of most of the other groups that have been incorporated into the United States over time. For true harmony between families and schools, the schools must understand the strengths as well as the limitations of collectivistic and individualistic value systems. They must understand what today's immigrants are giving up as well as what they are getting by adapting to the dominant North American society. We need to understand that there has been a continuing historical shift toward individualism in the United States, fueled by technological development, social movements, and decreasing family size. We also need to understand that this shift has its dysfunctional elements, such as alienation, loneliness, and violence. When we acknowledge these negative elements, we may be able to recognize the collectivism of recent immigrants as a much-needed balancing factor to the galloping individualism of U.S. society.

The best hope for children is for parents to work together with school personnel to establish academic and social goals, learning about and implementing
each other's (culture-based) values and expectations in the process. For this to
happen, the entire school system, including the administrative staff, must be dedicated to such mutual learning and genuinely open to real cross-cultural exchange
about practices and beliefs. As Comer and Haynes have said, parent involvement
programs "work best when they are based on child development concerns and
when they are implemented within a broader context of improved relationships
among the significant adults in the lives of children" (1991, p. 277). Of course it
takes effort to build strong relationships between school and home under any
circumstances. Schooling holds high stakes for all students; and parents and
professional educators, even those from the same cultural background, don't
always agree on educational goals or how to reach them. When major cultural
differences are layered on top of the usual challenges, the risk of conflict in goals
and methods increases. After all, culture exerts a mighty influence on how people
think about child-rearing, education, learning, knowledge, and schooling. What is
considered "normal" is simply what the majority culture thinks is normal and
accords a preferred status. When we use the word "mainstream," it really refers to
individualistic values of northern European and pioneer origin. "This fixing of the
'norm' yields a tension-filled relationship with those families and children not
included in that [interpretation of the norm]: the school can be a foreign, alienat-
ing, disrespectful place where nobody seems to 'care...' " (Dyson, 1997, p. 18). By
seeing alternative norms as a way to counter the weaknesses of the individualistic
system of education, we are respecting alternative value systems and can improve
education for all children and outcomes for society as a whole.

THE NEED FOR CULTURAL KNOWLEDGE

Comer's and Haynes' vision of improved relationships among all the significant
adults in a child's life would seem to rest on mutual respect and understanding,
along with revised ideas of what the range of "normal" can be. But such requirements are jeopardized (a) because of educators' relative lack of exposure to models for understanding how culture and schooling relate to each other, and (b)
teachers' lack of access to research based on these models. It is undoubtedly true
that schools will need to take the lead in nurturing stronger relationships with
families, but they will have greater success if they approach the task with some
grasp of the ways culture shapes views of child development and schooling. At
the very outset, they will need to make their own cultural perspectives visible,

something that is often more easily done by contrasting them to another perspective via a framework such as that of individualism / collectivism.

Reason for Optimism

The outcomes of the *Bridging Cultures Project* are cause for optimism. Some of the most striking ones have to do with (1) the perspective teachers have gained on their own culture and school culture, (2) the degree to which this has begun to influence their thinking and their practice in positive ways, and (3) the increased confidence teachers have in their own abilities to build the kinds of relationships with families that will support student success in school. They know how to learn from their students' families, and they have new ways of understanding what parents are sharing with them. What they have learned will stand them in good stead whenever they encounter students from unknown cultures, although the specifics will be different. We believe the project has been successful for the following reasons:

- It uses a theory- and research-based framework to guide empirical investigation.
- It has a committed group of teacher-researchers and staff researchers.
- It fills a gap in professional development and inquiry.
- It is not prescriptive but offers a generative framework.
- It offers opportunities to share and analyze practice.
- It includes meetings that incorporate both rigorous intellectual work and enjoyable interpersonal activities such as sharing meals, humor, and personal celebrations.

Indeed, the framework itself has proven more generative than we dreamed possible. There has been no end to the applications teachers have identified and innovations they have developed. Teachers can apply the framework in ways that make sense in their classrooms and schools and which they are comfortable with. As noted earlier, not all innovations are of equal value or success. They need to be evaluated in light of the framework and research, as well as tested by teachers, to see how they work and what outcomes they drive. There is no recommended mix of individualism and collectivism in the classroom; and although most of the innovations have, quite naturally, been in the direction of making uniformly individualistic classrooms more collectivistic, teachers recognize that neither system is all good or all bad. One teacher said, "I think that is a good point to bring out about culture… that… we're not saying collectivism is right, and individualism is wrong. We're just saying to recognize it. It's different." Others agreed.

UPDATE: WHAT'S HAPPENING NOW?

The *Bridging Cultures* team continues to meet periodically. At this point, we have begun to have "themed" meetings, where we discuss questions like, "How has *Bridging Cultures* affected your language arts instruction?" or "What do you think *Bridging Cultures* [meaning the framework] has to say regarding equitable assessment?" More recently, we have asked, "How can the framework help us understand and improve relations between African-American and Latino students and teachers?" To address this last question, we not only expanded our group of teachers but also read several articles and book chapters that African-American colleagues had recommended.

Questions like the ones above generate intense conversations with many examples and insights. It is always amazing to look back at the notes from a meeting (one staff researcher takes thorough notes to be shared with everyone later) and see how much has been covered in a matter of three or four hours. Two studies of classroom interaction have been carried out (Correa-Chavez, 1999; Isaac, 1999). Staff researchers are engaging in a new round of classroom visits and teacher interviews to attempt to capture and understand what teachers are doing in their classrooms — their newest research efforts — as a result of the project. Regional and national presentations continue. Publications are being prepared.

HOW DOES *BRIDGING CULTURES* FIT INTO THE BIG PICTURE OF SCHOOL REFORM?

We would like to step back and reflect on our own process of co-creating the project and writing this book and share some thoughts that rise to the surface again and again. Every single one of us involved in the project has a passionate belief in the value of promoting the best educational opportunities for all children. But we know that the discrepancy between what our schools offer so-called "mainstream" students and what they offer immigrant and other nondominant culture students is huge. So we are focused on improving opportunities for the latter students. We believe that our best hope for doing so lies in recognizing how our school practices perpetuate inequities. One factor, which can be addressed, is ignorance of the role of culture in schooling, child-rearing, and child development. Ignorance of how culture influences approaches to schooling and child-rearing leads to misunderstandings of why parents and children think and act the ways they do; it leads to maintenance of ineffective educational policies and strategies; and it ultimately leads to the loss of many students in our school system. We need to become true partners with parents. This entails taking the lead to understand their perspectives, helping to make the school's culture more visible (and, hence, potentially mutable) to everyone involved, and moving to change school culture to be more hospitable to students other than those from the dominant culture.

With regard to the move toward uniform standards and accountability procedures for all students, we must remember how important context is in providing excellence for the diverse population of students in U.S. schools. The goal of excellence for all students is, of course, a worthy goal. But when a single idea of what makes for high-quality schooling overwhelms the multiplicity of voices in our society, we know that the course of education is diminished and some students lose out. For example, many highly collectivistic cultures believe that a process of education quite naturally includes attention to social, moral, and ethical domains. Yet, to date the nationally developed content area standards, such as those for mathematics and language arts, do not address those elements at all. For some communities, such as many traditional American Indian societies, this constitutes a crucial oversight (Estrin & Nelson-Barber, 1995). Some of their most important values are missing in these "reform" documents. Yes, it is challenging for a multicultural society to craft goals and methods that meet the needs of all students, but the failure to take on this task has left many of our students and their families on the fringes of the enterprise of schooling.

The Bridge Metaphor

The bridge metaphor is a very rich one. The layers of analogy are myriad. In teaching her pre-service education students about the *Bridging Cultures* framework, one of us (Rothstein-Fisch) likes to say to them, "Enjoy the view from the bridge itself, with the ability to see both sides almost simultaneously." The bridge is more than just knowledge of each cultural framework. It is an expansion of understanding cultures *beyond that which can be seen only from one side or the other*. Frameworks such as individualism / collectivism help each of us to put our own culture in relief. At first we may exaggerate the contrasts between our culture and others or resist acknowledging that there are any differences at all. However, as we observe ourselves and others, we understand everyday interchanges and events in a new light. There is a personal dimension to all of this. It is not just understanding our students' urge to share, but also understanding our own tendencies to focus on individual achievement to the exclusion of other values in our classrooms. It's about a total shift from one way of seeing the home/school landscape to having perspectives from both sides of the cultural bridge.

Many of us in the project and others who have heard our presentations are struck with how differently we see the world, once we have new ways of doing so. We catch ourselves when we make one-sided judgments, and we hear others' comments or interpret their behavior differently. One *Bridging Cultures* teacher said "I think I'm a little more tolerant of who's in the parent conference — grandparents, siblings, etc. Also, this awareness has helped explain why Latino parents are there [in the school at breakfast time] for food, for the flag salute. Another teacher [commenting on the parents' behavior] said to me, 'That's why the students are immature...because parents stay until kids go into the classroom.' But I realize that it has to do with the importance of the family as a unit." All of us have developed the ability to move back and forth across the bridge a little more. Certainly, the burden of bridge travel will always be on those from nondominant cultures — those who attempt to fully live in two cultures — but we can all try to make the effort more mutual.

WHAT'S TO BE GAINED?

Where to begin? There is so much to be gained from cultural understanding and being able to act on it to change school practice. For starters, we are likely to have happier, more engaged, more successful students. These students are likely to have fewer conflicts between home and school, and their parents are more likely to become the kind of "involved" parents every decent school tries to cultivate. If we think in grander terms, we can see the kinds of changes *Bridging Cultures* teachers are making as contributing to a more democratic society, one that respects and responds to the needs of a far greater range of people. And many would argue that the inclusion of stronger values of community and caring for others (touchstones of collectivism) would represent a welcome shift in a society so focused on individuals. An educator and child development expert who has spent years in Japan observing in primary schools can no longer accept the almost exclusive emphasis on student achievement in United States schools. She says, "It is shocking to me how many school improvement efforts in the United States evaluate *only* whether a given program improves academic achievement — as though schools could somehow perform a surgical strike on children's intellects without profoundly shaping their social and ethical development. Critical to children's social and ethical development are close, trusting relationships with adults and children and opportunities to contribute to the well-being of others....Intentionally or not, school shapes children ethically, socially, and intellectually. Are *all three* considered in designing every feature of school life?" (Lewis, 1995, p. 209). Unlike individualism, the value framework of collectivism *does* consider all three in a more balanced way.

While the *Bridging Cultures* teachers have a major goal of helping their students maximize their achievement, they are also dedicated to positive relationships with their students and parents and among students. They do not see these

as separable elements: student achievement depends on a sense of belonging and
well-being in the classroom. This sense of belonging and well-being is dependent
on understanding and on avoiding unnecessary conflicts, pitting student, parent,
and teacher against each other. Figure 6.1 shows our conception of how outcomes
of *Bridging Cultures* can be expected to contribute to achievement. We see teachers' increased understanding, their change in stance toward parents and students,
and their resulting changes in practice — or rededication to culturally compatible

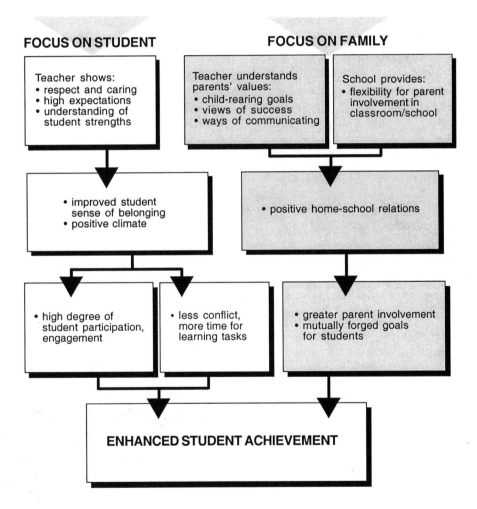

FOCUS ON STUDENT   **FOCUS ON FAMILY**

Teacher shows:
• respect and caring
• high expectations
• understanding of
  student strengths

Teacher understands
parents' values:
• child-rearing goals
• views of success
• ways of communicating

School provides:
• flexibility for parent
  involvement in
  classroom/school

• improved student
  sense of belonging
• positive climate

• positive home-school relations

• high degree of
  student participation,
  engagement

• less conflict,
  more time for
  learning tasks

• greater parent involvement
• mutually forged goals
  for students

ENHANCED STUDENT ACHIEVEMENT

Figure. 6.1
How Bridging Cultures Supports Conditions for Academic Achievement

practices they already engaged in — as establishing the necessary environment for student success. Of course, success may not be conceptualized in equivalent terms by all parents. Academic achievement, something that most policy-makers seem to embrace as the only important outcome of schooling, is only one aspect of success. Nevertheless, all students should be afforded the opportunity to achieve academically; and we know from considerable research that when classrooms do not engender a sense of belonging and foster student engagement, academic achievement suffers.

We hope we have been able to inspire and encourage our colleagues in education to find out what is to be gained in their settings by exploring these relationships between culture and schooling. Our experience has been that these ideas are so engaging, and the *Bridging Cultures* teachers' innovations so appealing, that teachers are willing to delve into applying the theory and research in their schools. We are also heartened by the number of folks in higher education who have found ways to include these ideas in their courses. Applying them does not really mean more work for teachers; it means working with the home culture of students and their families, instead of fighting against it. This strategy enables families to reap the benefits of schooling without sacrificing their own values. It avoids the tragedy of separating children from the culture of their parents and their home that subtly but consistently occurs.

But it is not just avoidance of tragedy that is gained: Important positive "goods" also result. When teachers stop trying to eradicate home values and begin to appreciate collectivistic behaviors and attitudes in their students, the school environment begins to support parents in socializing important "pro-social" qualities — qualities such as helpfulness, sharing, and family unity. Everyone agrees that these qualities are important, but they receive a much higher priority in a collectivistic value system than in an individualistic one. Given the historical trend toward increasing individualism in the U.S., it may be time to recognize these qualities as important, if not necessary, contributions to our society as a whole.

Questions for Reflection and Research

1. If you are already teaching, can you see ways of applying the *Bridging Cultures* framework to your own practice? How?
2. If you are not already teaching, how do you think you will apply the *Bridging Cultures* framework when you begin to teach?
3. What are your personal beliefs about the value of respecting and understanding students' home cultures? How do you reflect these in your teaching (or your thoughts and plans about teaching)?
4. How can understanding of students' home cultures be used to improve school reform efforts? Think of the specific initiatives your school or district has mounted and consider how cultural knowledge might make them more successful for students from nondominant cultures.

Further Reading

Bellah, R. N., Madsen, R., Sullivan, W.M., Swidler, A., & Tipton, S.M. (1991). *The good society*. New York: Alfred A. Knopf.

Lewis, C. C. *Educating hearts and minds*. (1995). Cambridge, England: Cambridge University Press.

McCaleb, S.P. (1997). *Building communities of learners: A collaboration among teachers, students, families, and community*. Mahwah, NJ: Lawrence Erlbaum Associates.

Appendix

The *Bridging Cultures Project* in Brief

Although it was clear to Patricia Greenfield and her colleagues that the individualism / collectivism framework was a cogent tool for understanding many conflict-ridden cross-cultural interactions in schools, it was *not* clear whether teachers would find it useful for solving problems in their schools and classrooms. Often teachers or teachers-in-training are exposed to interesting theories, but when they try to imagine what those theories mean in terms of what they should actually do in the classroom, they are left hanging. Could teachers benefit from understanding how these different value orientations motivate different expectations of children and of schools? The *Bridging Cultures Project* was founded to address this question. What is described here are primarily the initial design and outcomes of the *Project*.

BACKGROUND AND PURPOSE

The *Bridging Cultures Project* is a collaboration among a regional educational laboratory (WestEd), a research university (UCLA), a large teacher education institution (California State University, Northridge) and seven bilingual public school teachers from Southern California. The goal of the *Project* was to see if, and in what ways, the individualism / collectivism framework would be useful to teachers in identifying new strategies to build cross-cultural bridges in classrooms. Another purpose of the *Project* was to test the validity of a professional development process.

THE PEOPLE

Staff Researchers

A group of four researchers from the institutions named above came together: a cultural developmental psychologist, an applied psycholinguist, an educational psychologist/teacher-educator, and a Latin American Studies graduate student with a B.A. in psychology who is a former bilingual teacher. We represented the European-American and immigrant Latino populations whose school conflicts we would be addressing. We refer to this group as "staff researchers" to distinguish them from the teacher subjects who became *Bridging Cultures* researchers themselves.

Teachers

Seven elementary school bilingual teachers serving predominantly immigrant Latino families have participated in the *Project*. Four of the teachers are Latino/a; three are European-American. Two teachers were born in Mexico, one in Peru, and one in Germany, although all of these had immigrated to the United States as young children, between two and eight years of age. Three teachers were born in the United States.

Six female and one male teacher have participated in the *Project*. The teachers' grade assignments range from kindergarten to fifth grade, with every grade level represented by at least one teacher. This has remained true, even with changes in grade assignment, except for the 2000-01 school year. All teachers are bilingual (to varying degrees) in English and Spanish. The teachers were all experienced in their profession, with years of teaching ranging from 5 to 21 (mean=12.7) in the first year of the *Project*. The teachers were selected to participate on the basis of their demonstrated interest in better serving their immigrant Latino students.

PHASE I: PROCEDURES

The four staff researchers jointly designed and conducted three four-hour workshops, all taking place on Saturday mornings over a period of three months, September-December, 1996. The sessions were held in a small library at UCLA. A stipend of $300 was provided for each teacher participating in the three workshops. Each workshop was well documented, in videotape and in staff-recorded notes. All seven teachers and staff researchers were present at each workshop.

Workshop One

At the first meeting, after brief introductions, teachers responded to a pre-assessment consisting of a set of four scenarios describing home and school conflicts (two at school and two at home), that could be solved in several possible ways. The pre-assessment was designed to reveal the degree to which teachers already had awareness of individualism and collectivism as value orientations. The pretest presented scenarios validated in the initial study by Greenfield, Raeff & Quiroz (1996; 2000). Each scenario asked teachers to suggest solutions to conflicts under three conditions. Teachers first solved the scenario from their own perspective, then as they perceived an immigrant Latino parent might do so, and finally from the point of view of a European-American parent. The "Jobs Scenario," shown in Fig. 1.1 and already discussed, is one example of the scenarios used in the pre-test.

The teachers were given blank journals for recording observations of situations or behaviors in their schools and classrooms they perceived as related to individualism and collectivism throughout the training period. In addition, reading materials related to the theory and research on individualism and collectivism were distributed (Greenfield & Cocking, 1994). The teachers' assignment was to read more about the individualism / collectivism framework and to bring in examples of how this played out in the classroom to the subsequent workshop (Rothstein-Fisch, Trumbull, & Greenfield, 1999).

Workshop Two

At the second workshop, teachers returned to share their observations, discussing in small groups how the framework had helped them see themselves, their students, and their teaching in new ways. They met in three small groups, paired with one or two of the staff researchers who acted as scribes. The small group configuration afforded many opportunities for the teachers to describe their experiences and to verify their relationship to the framework of individualism and collectivism. For example, a teacher noted a striking contrast between her class and the class next door. She had her first grade children working in groups, while the other first grade teacher had her students working as individuals. When both teachers were called out into the hall for a quick meeting to arrange rainy day recess, the difference between the classes was obvious. The children working together maintained a consistent pattern of work with little attention to their teacher's absence. On the other hand, the children working individually became immediately disruptive and boisterous. The teacher wondered whether this was an example of the natural collectivistic inclination of immigrant Latino children.

One teacher remarked that now she is critical when teachers say there are "no differences" between children — they are "all the same." Another teacher said, "I feel as if a faucet has been turned on. I keep noticing things at home, at school. I can see things at home and school relating. Our staff was planning a 'math night' for showing the new math program to parents. Someone said, 'What about the kids?' We were working on the flyers, and one teacher said, 'Just write "No kids".' I said, 'That would be very uncultural.' " The question of whether teachers would find the framework useful was beginning to be answered. Like the first workshop, the second one, which extended well beyond the time scheduled, was full of animated discussion. At the end of the workshop, teachers were asked to make a change in their classroom applying the framework of individualism and collectivism. They also were asked to continue noting examples of individualism and collectivism in their journals.

Workshop Three

At the third workshop, teachers described what they had done in the intervening weeks to apply the *Bridging Cultures* framework in their classrooms and schools. It was at this meeting that teachers began talking about how they used helpers in their classrooms. One teacher said she was not just allowing children to help each other; she was actively encouraging it. Another noted the irony of having social studies curriculum goals of getting along with others (social skills) but not encouraging this kind of helping routinely. The first teacher said, "You can do that goal and do it individualistically," suggesting that individualistic values would still prevail to limit the kind and amount of helping that might take place. The second teacher noted that she was taking a new approach with "Math Their Way," letting students help each other and acknowledging that "two heads are better than one." Discussion at this meeting was rapid-fire and showed that teachers were using the framework to guide a great deal of thinking about interpersonal relations and instruction in the classroom.

Teachers also completed a post-assessment to be used to compare their initial understanding of the framework with their understanding after some exposure to the theory and experience using the framework to observe their own students and themselves and to modify classroom practice. In addition, teachers completed a detailed questionnaire to evaluate the professional development process and the usefulness of what they had learned. As part of the questionnaire, teachers were asked: "Will you use your knowledge of individualism and collectivism in your classroom? If so, how?"

WORKSHOP OUTCOMES

Pre-and Post-Test Assessment

Their responses to the pre-assessment questionnaire and the discussion that followed showed that individualistic assumptions guided teachers' ideal methods of problem solving and that they were unaware of an alternative frame of reference. As in the prior research, there were no differences between Latina/o and European-American teachers on this dimension (Raeff, Greenfield, & Quiroz, 2000). Teachers discussed their responses to the scenarios as a whole group.

Teachers' responses on the pre-assessment and post-assessment were analyzed according to a protocol developed for previous research (Raeff, Greenfield, & Quiroz, 2000). Their responses to scenarios such as that shown in Chapter 1 changed dramatically from more individualistic to more collectivistic (see Table A.1) (Rothstein-Fisch, Trumbull, Quiroz, & Greenfield, 1997). The totals of 14 in each column represent the seven teachers' responses to two scenarios for which high reliability of scoring was established in the previous research. Although there was no change in their perception of the Latino or European-American parent perspective, the outcome for the teachers was a more balanced orientation between the two value systems. This balance was achieved by adding acceptance of the collectivistic mode to their prior preference for the individualistic perspective.

Other Outcomes

Over lunch, the group talked about its future as well as what individual teachers might do with the framework. They shared ideas about classroom changes they were planning. They also put new emphasis on their relationships with parents. Moreover, they discussed ways to move the framework into other professional development activities with which they were involved, such as their work as mentor teachers. Ideas for carrying the *Project* forward — beyond the initial workshops — were initiated by the teachers themselves. They suggested promoting the framework within their schools.

At the conclusion of the third and final workshop, teachers were unanimous in their suggestion to continue meeting and working together. They found that the framework was altering their perceptions of interactions in the classroom and of

interactions between parents and school. They wanted to keep talking and thinking as a group, and they agreed to participate in developing materials and presentations based on the *Bridging Cultures* framework of individualism and collectivism. As one teacher said later, "Meeting three times sets the fire, but nothing's
been cooked yet. The risks are that people will go back and close the door on their
classrooms. We should keep this core group alive."

PHASE II: CHANGES IN TEACHERS' ROLES

As of the conclusion of the third workshop, teachers began to shift their role from
teacher-subject to collaborator and teacher-researcher. In these new roles, they
have advanced the *Bridging Cultures Project* in many ways. First, they have
continued to test the validity and usefulness of the theoretical framework, applying explicit knowledge of individualism and collectivism in daily life and in their
school communities. In the process they have developed and documented numerous innovations that bridge cultures for children and families (Quiroz, Greenfield,
& Altchech, 1999; Rothstein-Fisch, Greenfield, & Trumbull, 1999; Trumbull, Rothstein-Fisch, & Greenfield, 2000). Second, teachers have actively participated in
planning and disseminating the *Project*. They have co-designed and presented
workshops and conference presentations, developed presentation handouts, and
contributed to *Project*-related publications. Third, teachers have been pivotal to
the process of deciding on the most productive routes of dissemination within the
Los Angeles Unified School District, a particularly important "market" because of
its size, numbers of new and inexperienced teachers, and large immigrant Latino
student population. In addition, discussions during meetings have often included

Table A.1

Changes in teachers' orientation to problem solving based on individualism and collectivism

value orientation	pre-assessment	post-assessment
individualistic	12	3
collectivistic	1	8
both	0	3
neither	1	0

(from Rothstein-Fisch, Trumbull, Quiroz, & Greenfield, 1997) how the teachers could reach other teachers in their schools, to share what they are learning. Teachers have also given several workshops in their own schools.

DOCUMENTING TEACHER CHANGE

Throughout the past four years, the *Bridging Cultures* group has met on Saturdays approximately every two months. Two of the staff researchers, who are also university professors, have included some of their students in the meetings because of their research interests in the *Project*. Several of these students have based B.A. and M.A. theses on their research into *Bridging Cultures* (Correa-Chavez, 1999; Geary, in preparation; Jun, 2000; Isaac, 1999), and one has co-authored a conference paper that will be published (Trumbull, Greenfield, Rothstein-Fisch, & Maynard, 1999). In the post-workshop training meetings, teachers have continued their enthusiastic and lengthy discussions about what they are observing and how their new perspective has affected their instruction and interactions with children, parents, and other teachers. They have continued to keep notes on applications of the framework for group discussion.

In addition to documenting teachers' changes described in the meetings, staff researchers have observed all seven teachers in their classrooms at least twice for durations of from two hours to half a day. In some cases, graduate students from California State University, Northridge or UCLA have conducted observations. After each observation, researchers interviewed the teacher, exploring questions arising from the observation. The open-ended post-observation interviews, usually lasting over one hour, have led to a deeper understanding of how teachers conceptualize their instructional practice and new insights into their relationship with student and parents. Throughout the observation and debriefing process, the emphasis has been on how the framework of individualism and collectivism has influenced the teachers' thinking, practice, and educational outcomes. The theme of home-school relations, which was magnified as teachers approached a round of parent-teacher conferences and read a paper on cross-cultural parent-teacher conferences (Greenfield, Raeff, & Quiroz, 1998), emerged as the focus for this *Guide*, in part from this process of observations and interviews.

A second round of extended interviews was conducted in early 2000 to capture teachers' reflections and analyses after more than three years of involvement in the *Project*. These interviews show in even greater depth teachers' understanding of the implications of the individualism / collectivism framework, along with many additional examples of ongoing changes in relationships and instructional practice. Teachers demonstrate in these interviews an appreciation for both the power and the limitations of the framework; they see the framework as a tool for developing cultural understanding that influences their pedagogy, but they also see the complexities of individual lives and the dangers of making assumptions about people on the basis of generalizations. One teacher commented that it is dangerous to "lump people together" on the basis of the framework. She also observed that "...there are so many microcultures within the macroculture, and people in certain areas of a country have a completely different cultural value or belief than in another area of the country." Another said, " The framework may be more apropos for the immigrants. The parents start to take on new roles and their own culture is starting to fade. The parents have been here a while. The families have been exposed to the media and other teachers' input. They have been to parent classes or 'parenting classes,' so to speak, to learn 'what their role should be here'." These comments show that teachers are using the framework critically.

POWERFUL EXAMPLES MAKE THE FRAMEWORK COME ALIVE

What made the *Bridging Cultures Project* workshops so successful? Teachers reported that they could grasp the invisible cultural values of immigrants because a series of examples of individualism and collectivism clearly illustrated familiar home-school conflicts. Indeed, the *Bridging Cultures Project* relied heavily on real-life examples from the field, making explicit how individualistic assumptions on the part of a teacher do not fit the characteristics of collectivistic learners (Greenfield, Rothstein-Fisch, & Quiroz, 1999). Many of these examples, along with "deconstruction" of their meanings from the perspective of the individualism / collectivism framework, are included in this *Guide*.

Teachers have used the examples to aid their own creative problem solving. Lessons learned from these examples seem to generate awareness both of cultural values conflicts and of new ways to build bridges between cultures.

References

Abrahams, R. D. (1970). *Deep down in the jungle: Negro narratives from the streets of Philadelphia* (Rev. ed.), Chicago: Aldine.

Allexsaht-Snider, M. (1992, April). *Bilingual parents' perspectives on home-school linkages.* Paper presented at the Annual Meeting of the American Educational Research Association, San Francisco, CA.

Allexsaht-Snider, M. (1995). Teachers' perspectives on their work with families in a bilingual community. *Journal of Research in Childhood Education,* 9(2), 95-96.

Aronson, J. Z. (1996). How schools can recruit hard-to-reach parents. *Educational Leadership,* 53(7), 58–60.

Artiles, A. J. (1996). Teacher thinking in urban schools. In F.A. Rios (Ed.), *Teacher thinking in cultural contexts* (pp. 23–52). Albany, NY: State University of New York Press.

Au, K. (1980). Participation structures in a reading lesson with Hawaiian children: Analysis of a culturally appropriate instructional event. *Anthropology and Education Quarterly,* 11(2), 91–115.

Au, K. H., & Kawakami, A. J. (1994). Cultural congruence in instruction. In E. R. Hollins, J. E. King, & W. G. Hayman (Eds.), *Teaching diverse populations: Formulating a knowledge base* (pp. 5–23). Albany, NY: State University of New York Press.

Banks, J. A. (1995). Multicultural education: Historical development, dimensions, and practice. In J.A. Banks (Ed.), *Handbook of research on multicultural education* (pp. 3–24). New York: Macmillan Publishing USA.

Barth, R.S. (1990). *Improving schools from within*. San Francisco, CA: Jossey-Bass.

Blake, I. K. (1994). Language development and socialization in young African-American children. In P. M. Greenfield & R. R. Cocking (Eds.), *Cross-cultural roots of minority child development* (pp. 167–195). Hillsdale, NJ: Lawrence Erlbaum Associates.

Brislin, R. (1993). *Understanding culture's influence on behavior*. Fort Worth, TX: Harcourt Brace College Publishers.

Brown, R. (1957). *Words and things*. Glencoe, IL: Free Press.

Burnaford, G. (1996). Supporting teacher research: Professional development and the reality of schools. In G. Burnaford, J. Fischer, & D. Hobson (Eds.), *Teachers doing research: Practical possibilities* (pp. 137–150). Mahwah, NJ: Lawrence Erlbaum Associates.

Burnaford, G., Fischer, J., & Hobson, D. (1996). *Teachers doing research: Practical possibilities*. Mahwah, NJ: Lawrence Erlbaum Associates.

Calfee, R., Whittaker, A., Wolf, S., & Wong, I. (1989, April). *The inquiring school: Staff development and evaluation through collaboration*. Paper presented at the Annual Meeting of the American Educational Research Association, San Francisco, CA.

Calhoun, E. F. (1993). Action research: Three approaches. *Educational Leadership*, 51(2), 62–65.

California Department of Education, Bilingual Education Office. (1994). *Handbook for teaching Vietnamese-speaking students*. Sacramento, CA: California Department of Education Press.

Carey, N., Lewis, L., & Farris, E. (1998). *Parent involvement in children's education: Efforts by public elementary schools*. Washington, DC: National Center for Education Statistics, U.S. Department of Education, Office of Educational Research and Improvement.

Casanova, U. (1996). Parent involvement: A call for prudence. *Educational Researcher*, 25(8), 30–32, 46.

Cazden, C. B., & Leggett. E. L. (1981). Culturally responsive education: Recommendations for achieving Lau remedies II. In H. Trueba, G. Guthrie, & K. Au (Eds.), *Culture and the bilingual classroom*. Rowley, MA: Newbury House.

Center on Organization and Restructuring of Schools (Winter, 1994). *Brief to principals* (Brief No. 8). Madison, WI: University of Michigan, School of Education.

Chavkin, N. F. (1989). Debunking the myth about minority parents. *Educational Horizons*, 67(4), 119–123.

Chavkin, N. F., & Williams, D. L. (1993). Minority parents and the elementary school: Attitudes and practices. In N. F. Chavkin (Ed.), *Families and schools in a pluralistic society* (pp. 73–83). New York: State University of New York Press.

Chavkin, N. F. (Ed.) (1993). *Families and schools in a pluralistic society*. New York: State University of New York Press.

Choi, S. C., Kim, U., & Choi, S. H. (1993). Korean culture and collective representation. In U. Kim & J. W. Berry (Eds.), *Indigenous psychologies: Experience and research in cultural context* (pp. 193–210). Newbury Park, CA: Sage.

Chrispeels, J. (1988). Building collaboration through parent-teacher conferencing. *Educational Horizons*, 66(2), 87–89.

Cochran, M., & Dean, C. (1991). Home-school relations and the empowerment process. *The Elementary School Journal*, 91(3), 261–269.

Cochran-Smith, M., & Lytle, S. L. (1993). *Inside/outside: Teacher research and knowledge* (pp. 27–88). New York: Teachers College Press.

Cochran-Smith, M. (1997). Knowledge, skills, and experiences for teaching culturally diverse learners: A perspective for practicing teachers. In J. J. Irvine (Ed.), *Critical knowledge for diverse teachers and learners* (pp. 27–87). Washington, DC: American Association of Colleges for Teacher Education.

Cochran-Smith, M., & Lytle, S. L. (1999). The teacher research movement: A decade later. *Educational Researcher*, 28(7), 15–25.

Coles, R. (1989). *The call of stories: Teaching and the moral imagination*. Boston, MA: Houghton-Mifflin.

Comer, J. P., & Haynes, N. M. (1991). Parent involvement in schools: An ecological approach. *The Elementary School Journal*, 91(3), 271–277.

Connors, L. J., & Epstein, J. L. (1995). Parent and school partnerships. In M. H. Bornstein (Ed.), *Handbook of parenting* Vol 4: *Applied and Practical Parenting* (pp. 437–458). Mahwah, NJ: Lawrence Erlbaum Associates.

Correa-Chavez, M. (1999). Bridging Cultures *between home and school: Assessment of an intervention program*. Unpublished manuscript, Psychology Honors Thesis, UCLA, Los Angeles, CA.

Cuban, L. (1992). Managing dilemmas while building professional communities. *Educational Researcher*, 21(1), 4–11.

Dauber, S. L., & Epstein, J. L. (1993). Parents' attitudes and practices of involvement in inner-city elementary and middle schools. In N. F. Chavkin (Ed.), *Families and schools in a pluralistic society* (pp. 53–71). New York: State University of New York Press.

Davies, D. (1991, January). Schools reaching out: Family, school, and community partnerships for student success. *Phi Delta Kappan*, 72(5), 376–382.

Dead poets society (1989). Touchstone Pictures.

De Kanter, A, Ginsburg, A. L., Pederson, J., Peterson, T. K., & Rich, D. (1997). *A compact for learning: An action handbook for family-school-community partnerships*. Washington, DC: U.S. Department of Education.

Delgado-Gaitan, C. (1990). *Literacy for empowerment*. New York: The Falmer Press.

Delgado-Gaitan, C. (1991). Involving parents in the schools: A process of empowerment. *American Journal of Education*, 100, 20–46.

Delgado-Gaitan, C. (1992). School matters in the Mexican American home: Socializing children to education. *American Educational Research Journal*, 29, 495–513.

Delgado-Gaitan, C., & Segura, D. (1989). The social context of Chicana women's role in children's schooling. *Educational Foundations*, 3, 71–92.

Delgado-Gaitan, C. (1994). Socializing young children in Mexican-American families: An intergenerational perspective. In P.M. Greenfield & R. R. Cocking (Eds.), *Cross-cultural roots of minority child development* (pp. 55–86). Hillsdale, NJ: Lawrence Erlbaum Associates.

Derman-Sparks, L., Phillips, C. B., & Hilliard, III, A. G. (1997). *Teaching/learning anti-racism: A developmental approach*. New York: Teachers College Press.

Developmental Studies Center (1995). *Homeside activities*. Oakland, CA: Developmental Studies Center.

Dewey, J. (1933). *How we think*. Chicago: Henry Regnery.

Diaz, R. (2000). *Latina parent educational participation: A pro-active approach*. Unpublished dissertation, UCLA, Los Angeles, CA.

Dinkelman, T. (1997). The promise of action research for critically reflective teacher education. *Teacher Educator*, 32(4), 250–274.

Donoahue, Z., Van Tassell, M. A., & Patterson, L. (Eds.), (1996). *Reading in the classroom: Talk, texts, and inquiry*. Newark, DE: International Reading Association.

Duckworth, E. (1987). Teaching as research. In E. Duckworth, *"The having of wonderful ideas" and other essays* (pp. 122–140). New York: Teachers College Press.

Dyson, A. H., with the San Francisco East Bay Teacher Study Group (1997). *What difference does difference make? Teacher reflections on diversity, literacy, and the urban primary school*. Urbana, IL: National Council of Teachers of English.

Eggen, P., & Kauchak, D. (1997). *Educational psychology: Windows on classrooms* (3rd ed.). Upper Saddle River, NJ: Merrill/Prentice Hall.

Epstein, J. (1989). Family structures and student motivation: A developmental perspective. In C. Ames & R. Ames (Eds.), *Research on motivation in education*: Vol. 3. *Goals and cognitions* (pp. 259–295). New York: Academic Press.

Epstein, J. (1991). Effects on student achievement of teachers' practices of parent involvement. In S. B. Silvern (Ed.), *Advances in reading/language research: Vol. 5. Literacy through family, community, and school interaction* (pp. 261–276). Greenwich, CT: JAI Press.

Epstein, J. (1993). Make parents your partners. *Instructor*, 102, 52–53.

Epstein, J. (1994). *Perspectives and previews on research and policy for school, family, and community partnerships*. Paper presented at the Family-School Links Conference, Pennsylvania State University, PA.

Epstein, J. L., & Becker, H. J. (1982). Teacher practices of parent involvement: Problems and possibilities. *Elementary School Journal*, 83, 103–113.

Epstein, J. (1986). Parents' reactions to teacher practices of parent involvement. *Elementary School Journal*, 86, 277–294.

Epstein, J. L. (1998a, April). *Interactive homework: Effective strategies to connect home and school*. Paper presented at the Annual Meeting of the American Educational Research Association, San Diego, CA.

Epstein, J. (1998b, Fall). Sharing the role of expert in the National Network of Partnership Schools. *Type 2, National Network of Partnership Schools*. Baltimore: MD: Johns Hopkins University.

Estrin, E. T., & Nelson-Barber, S. (1995). *Issues in cross-cultural assessment: American Indian and Alaska Native students* (Knowledge Brief No. 12). San Francisco: Far West Laboratory for Educational Research and Development.

Fetterman, D. M. (1988). *Ethnography step by step. Applied Social Research Methods Series: Vol. 17*. Newbury Park, CA: Sage Publications.

Finders, M., & Lewis, C. (1994). Why some parents don't come to school. *Educational Leadership*, 51(8), 50–54.

Fine, M. (1993). [Ap]parent involvement: Reflections on parents, power, and urban public schools. *Teachers College Record*, 94, 682–710.

Florio-Ruane, S. (1991). Conversation and narrative in collaborative research: An ethnography of the written literacy forum. In C. Witherell & N. Noddings (Eds.), *Stories lives tell: Narrative and dialogue in education* (pp. 234–256). New York: Teachers College Press.

Freedman, S. W., Simons, E. R., Kalnin, J. S., Casareno, A., & The M-CLASS Teams. (1999). *Inside city schools: Investigating literacy in multicultural classrooms*. New York: Teachers College Press; and Urbana, IL: National Council of Teachers of English.

Freedman, S. W., with Wood, W., Austin, G., McFarland, B. L., & Potestio, P. (1999). What teacher researchers say about seeing beyond stereotypes. In S. W. Freedman, E. R. Simons, J S. Kalnin, A. Casareno, & the M-CLASS Teams, *Inside city schools: Investigating literacy in multicultural classrooms* (pp. 89–106). New York: Teachers College Press.

Freire, P. (1970). *Pedagogy of the oppressed.* New York: Seabury Press.

Garcia, S. B., Guerra, P. L., with Alsobrook, M. E. (2000, April). *Through their eyes: Educators' reflections about staff development on intercultural communication in the classroom.* Paper presented at the Annual Meeting of the American Educational Research Association. New Orleans, LA.

Gandara, P. C. (1995). *Over the ivy walls: The educational mobility of low-income Chicanos.* New York: State University of New York Press.

Geary, J.P. (in preparation). Bridging Cultures *through School Counseling: Theoretical understanding and practical solutions.* Unpublished master's thesis, Department of Educational Psychology and Counseling, California State University, Northridge, Northridge, CA.

Goals 2000: Educate America Act, Sec. 102 National Education Goals, (8) Parental Participation (1994).

Goldenberg, C., & Gallimore, R. (1995). Immigrant Latino parents' values and beliefs about their children's education: Continuities and discontinuities across cultures and generations. In P. Pintrich & M. Maehr (Eds.), *Advances in achievement motivation.* Vol. 9 (pp. 183–228). Greenwich, CT: JAI Press.

Goodman, Y. (1985). Kid watching: Observing children in the classroom. In A. Jaggar and M. T. Smith-Burke (Eds.), *Observing the language learner* (pp. 9–13). Urbana, IL: National Council of Teachers of English; and Newark, DE: International Reading Association.

Goodnow, J. J., & Collins, W. A. (1990). *Development according to parents: The nature, sources, and consequences of parents' ideas.* Hove, U.K.: Lawrence Erlbaum Associates.

Gorman, J. C., & Balter, L. (1997). Culturally sensitive parent education: A critical review of quantitative research. *Review of Educational Research*, 67(3), 339–369.

Goswami, P., & Stillman, P. (1987). *Reclaiming the classroom: Teacher research as an agency for change.* Upper Montclair, NJ: Boynton/Cook.

Greenfield, P., & Cocking, R. (Eds.). (1994). *Cross cultural roots of minority child development.* Hillsdale, NJ: Lawrence Erlbaum Associates.

Greenfield, P. M. (1994). Independence and interdependence as developmental scripts: Implications for theory, research and practice. In P. Greenfield & R. Cocking (Eds.), *Cross-cultural roots of minority child development* (pp. 1–37). Hillsdale, NJ: Lawrence Erlbaum Associates.

Greenfield, P. M., Brazelton, B., & Childs, C. (1989). From birth to maturity in Zinacantan: Ontogenesis in cultural context. In V. Bricker & G. Gossen (Eds.), *Ethnographic encounters in Southern Mesoamerica: Celebratory essays in honor of Evon Z. Vogt* (pp. 177–216). Albany, NY: Institute of Mesoamerican Studies, State University of New York.

Greenfield, P.M., Quiroz, B., & Raeff, C. (1996). Unpublished data.

Greenfield, P. M., Quiroz, B., & Raeff, C. (2000). Cross-cultural conflict and harmony in the social construction of the child. In S. Harkness, C. Raeff, & C.M. Super (Eds.), *Variability in the social construction of the child* (pp. 93–108). *New Directions in Child Development,* No. 87. San Francisco: Jossey-Bass.

Greenfield, P. M., Raeff, C., & Quiroz, B. (1996). Cultural values in learning and education. In B. Williams (Ed.), *Closing the achievement gap: A vision for changing beliefs and practices* (pp. 37–55). Alexandria, VA: Association for Supervision and Curriculum Development.

Greenfield, P. M., Raeff, C., & Quiroz, B. (1998). Cross-cultural conflict in the social construction of the child. *Aztlan, 23,* 115–125.

Greenfield, P. M., Rothstein-Fisch, C., & Quiroz, B. (1999, April). Bridging cultures *in education: Implicit knowledge through explicit training.* Paper presented at the meeting of the Society for Research in Child Development, Albuquerque, NM.

Greenfield, P. M., & Suzuki, L. (1998). Culture and human development: Implications for parenting, education, pediatrics, and mental health. In W. Damon (Ed.-in-Chief) & I. E. Sigel & K. A. Renninger (Vol. Eds.), *Handbook of Child Psychology:* 5th ed., Vol. 4 (pp. 1059–1108). New York: Wiley.

Guskey, T. (1986). Staff development and the process of teacher change. *Educational Researcher,* 15(4), 5–12.

Hall, E. (1959). *The silent language.* Garden City, NY: Doubleday.

Hall, E. (1966). *The hidden dimension.* Garden City, NY: Doubleday.

Hall, E. (1976). *Beyond culture.* Garden City, NY: Anchor Books.

Harkness, S., & Super, C. M. (Eds.) (1992). *Parents' cultural belief systems: Their origins, expressions, and consequences.* New York: Guilford Press.

Hattrup, R. A., & Bickel, W. F. (1993). Teacher-researcher collaborations: Resolving the tensions. *Educational Leadership,* 50(6), 38–41.

Heath, S. B. (1983). *Ways with words: Language, life, and work in communities and classrooms.* New York: Cambridge University Press.

Henderson, A. T., & Berla, N. (1994). *A new generation of evidence: The family is critical to student achievement.* Washington, DC: National Committee for Citizens in Education.

Hill, R. B. (1972). *The strengths of Black families.* New York: Emerson Hall.

Hobson, D. (1996). Learning with each other: Collaboration in teacher research. In G. Burnaford, J. Fischer, & D. Hobson (Eds.), *Teachers doing research: Practical possibilities* (pp. 93–108). Mahwah, NJ: Lawrence Erlbaum Associates.

Hofstede, G. (1983). National cultures revisited. *Behavior Science Research,* 18(4), 285-305.

Hollins, E. R. (1996). *Culture in school learning.* Mahwah, NJ: Lawrence Erlbaum Associates.

Hoover-Dempsey, K. V., & Sandler, H. M. (1997). Why do parents become involved in their children's education? *Review of Educational Research,* 67(1), 3–42.

Improving America's Schools Act, HR 6, 103rd Cong., 2nd Sess. (1994).

Ingvarson, L. (1987). *Models of inservice education and their implications for professional development policy.* Paper presented at a conference on Inservice Education: Trends of the Past, Themes for the Future, Melbourne, Australia.

Isaac, A. R. (1999). *How teachers' cultural ideologies influence children's relations inside the classroom: The effect of a cultural awareness teacher training program in two classrooms.* Unpublished manuscript, Psychology Honors Thesis, UCLA, Los Angeles, CA.

John, V. P. (1972). Styles of learning—styles of teaching: Reflections on the education of Navajo children. In C. B. Cazden, V. P. John, & D. Hymes (Eds.), *Functions of language in the classroom* (pp. 331–343). New York: Teachers College Press.

Joy luck club, the (1993). Buena Vista Studios.

Joyce, B.R. (1991). Doors to school improvement. *Educational Leadership, 48*(8), 59–62.

Joyce, B., & Calhoun, E. (1995). School renewal: An inquiry, not a formula. *Educational Leadership,* 52 (7), 51–55.

Jun, C. (2000). Bridging cultures *through school counselor education.* Unpublished master's thesis, California State University, Northridge, Northridge, CA.

Kalnin, J. S., Freedman, S. W., & Simons, E. R. (1999). Learning from M-CLASS: Thoughts for the future. In S. W. Freedman, E. R. Simons, J. S. Kalnin, A. Casareno, & The M-CLASS Teams. *Inside city schools: Investigating literacy in multicultural classrooms.* New York: Teachers College Press; and Urbana, IL: National Council of Teachers of English.

Kidder, T. (1989). *Among schoolchildren.* Boston, MA: Houghton-Mifflin.

Killion, J. P., & Todnem, G. R. (1991). A process for personal theory building. *Educational Leadership,* 48(6), 14–16.

Kim, U., & Choi, S. (1994). Individualism, collectivism, and child development: A Korean perspective. In P. M. Greenfield & R. Cocking (Eds.), *Cross-cultural roots of minority child development* (pp. 227–257). Hillsdale, NJ: Lawrence Erlbaum Associates.

King, J. E. (1994). The purpose of schooling for African American children: Including cultural knowledge. In E. R. Hollins, J. E. King, & W. C. Hayman (Eds.), *Teaching diverse populations; Formulating a knowledge base* (pp. 25–56). Albany, NY: State University of New York Press.

Kleinfeld, J. S. (1970). *Cognitive strengths of Eskimos and implications for education* (ISEGR Occasional Paper No. 3). Fairbanks, AK: Institute of Social, Economic and Government Research, University of Alaska.

Klimes-Dougan, B., Lopez, J. A., Nelson, P., & Adelman. H. S. (1992). Two studies of low income parents' involvement in schooling. *The Urban Review*, 24(3), 185–202.

Koelsch, N., & Estrin, E.T. (1996). Portfolios: Bridging cultural and linguistic worlds. In R.C. Calfee & P. Perfumo (Eds.), *Writing portfolios in the classroom: Policy and practice, promise and peril* (pp. 261–284). Mahwah, NJ: Lawrence Erlbaum Associates.

Ladson-Billings, G. (1991). *Distorting democracy: Social studies curriculum development and textbook adoption in California*. Paper presented at the meeting of the National Council for the Social Studies, Washington, DC.

Lieberman, A., & Miller, L. (1990). Teacher development in professional practice schools. *Teachers College Record*, 92(1), 105–122.

Lewis, C. C. (1995). *Educating hearts and minds*. Cambridge, England: Cambridge University Press.

Lipka, J., with Mohatt, G. V., & The Ciulistet Group (Eds.), (1998). *Transforming the culture of schools: Yup'ik Eskimo examples*. Mahwah, NJ: Lawrence Erlbaum Associates.

Lipka, J., & Yanez, E. (1998). Identifying and understanding cultural differences: Toward a culturally based pedagogy. In J. Lipka, with G. V. Mohatt and The Ciulistet Group (Eds.), *Transforming the culture of schools: Yup'ik Eskimo examples* (pp. 111–138). Mahwah, NJ: Lawrence Erlbaum Associates.

Little, J.W. (1993). Teachers' professional development in a climate of educational reform. *Educational Evaluation and Policy Analysis*, 15(2), 129–152.

Lucas, T., Henze, R., & Donato, R. (1990). Promoting the success of Latino language-minority students: An exploratory study of six high schools. *Harvard Educational Review*, 60(3), 315–340.

Lustig, M., & Koester, J. (1999). *Intercultural competence: Interpersonal communication across cultures*. New York: Longman Press.

McAdoo, H. (1978). Factors related to stability in upwardly mobile Black families. *Journal of Marriage and the Family*, 40, 762–778.

McCaleb, S. P. (1997). *Building communities of learners: A collaboration among teachers, students, families, and community*. Mahwah, NJ: Lawrence Erlbaum Associates.

McLaren, P. (1989). *Life in schools*. New York: Longman.

McLaughlin, M. W. (1990). The Rand change agent study revisited: Macro perspectives and micro realities. *Educational Researcher*, 19(9), 11–16.

Mesa-Bains, A. (1997). Commentary. In B. Farr & E. Trumbull. *Assessment alternatives for diverse classrooms* (pp. 28–33). Norwood, MA: Christopher-Gordon Publishers, Inc.

Mi famlia (1995). New Line.

Michaels, S. (1981). "Sharing time," Children's narrative styles and differential access to literacy. *Language in Society*, 10, 423–442.

Moles, O. C. (1993). Collaboration between schools and disadvantaged parents: Obstacles and openings. In N. F. Chavkin (Ed.), *Families and schools in a pluralistic society* (pp. 21–49). New York: State University of New York Press.

Moles, O. C. (Ed.) (1996). *Reaching all families: Creating family-friendly schools.* Washington, DC: Office of Educational Research and Improvement.

Moll, L. C., & Greenberg, J. (1991). Creating zones of possibilities: Combining social contexts for instruction. In L.C. Moll (Ed.), *Vygotsky and education* (pp. 319–348). Cambridge, England: Cambridge University Press.

More, A. J. (1989, August). Native Indian learning styles: A review for researchers and teachers. *Journal of American Indian Education*, special issue, 15–28.

Morris, V. G., Taylor, S. I., Knight, J., & Wasson, R. (1995). *Preparing preservice teachers to take leadership roles in parent involvement programs in schools.* Paper presented at the Annual Meeting of the Association of Teacher Educators, Detroit, MI.

Mundy-Castle, A. C. (1974). Social and technological intelligence in Western and non-Western cultures. *Universitas*, 4, 46–52.

National Education Goals Panel (1995). *Building a nation of learners.* Washington, DC: National Education Goals Panel.

Nelson-Barber, S., & Dull, V. (1998). Don't act like a teacher! Images of effective instruction in a Yup'ik Eskimo classroom. In J. Lipka (Ed.), with G. V. Mohatt & The Ciulistet Group. *Transforming the culture of schools: Yup'ik Eskimo examples* (pp. 91–105). Mahwah, NJ: Lawrence Erlbaum Associates.

Nieto, S. (1996). *Affirming diversity: The sociopolitical context of multicultural education.* New York: Longman.

Oja, S.N., & Smulyan, L. (1989). *Collaborative action research: A developmental approach.* London: Falmer Press.

Okagaki, L., & Sternberg, R. J. (1993). Parental beliefs and children's school performance. *Child Development*, 64, 36–56.

Onikama, D.L., Hammond, O. W., & Koki, S. (1998). *Family involvement in education: A synthesis of research for Pacific educators.* Honolulu, HI: Pacific Resources for Education and Learning.

Oregon State Department of Education (1990). *Parent involvement: The critical link.* Salem, OR: Oregon State Department of Education.

Pacific Mathematics and Science Leadership Team (1995, September). *Pacific stan-*

dards for excellence in teaching, assessment and professional development. Honolulu, HI: Pacific Mathematics and Science Regional Consortium, Pacific Region Educational Laboratory.

Pagano, J. (1991). Moral fictions: The dilemma of theory and practice. In C. Witherell & N. Noddings (Eds.), *Stories lives tell: Narrative and dialogue in education* (pp. 234–256). New York: Teachers College Press.

Pérez, A.I. (1995). Critical pedagogy: The voice of a classroom teacher. In J. Frederikson (Ed.), *Reclaiming our voices: Bilingual education, critical pedagogy and praxis* (pp. 225–240). Ontario, CA: California Association for Bilingual Education.

Quiroz, B., & Greenfield, P. M. (1996). *Cross-cultural values conflict: Removing a barrier to Latino school achievement.* Unpublished manuscript.

Quiroz, B., Greenfield, P. M., & Altchech, M. (1998, Winter). *Bridging Cultures between home and school: The parent-teacher conference. Connections*, 1, 8–11.

Quiroz, B., Greenfield, P. M., & Altchech, M. (1999). *Bridging Cultures* with a parent-teacher conference. *Educational Leadership*, 56(7), 68–70.

Raeff, C, Greenfield, P. M., & Quiroz, B. (2000). Conceptualizing interpersonal relationships in the cultural contexts of individualism and collectivism. In S. Harkness, C. Raeff, & C. Super (Eds.), *Variability in the social construction of the child.* (pp. 59–74). *New Directions in Child Development.* No. 87. San Francisco: Jossey-Bass.

Raeff, C., Greenfield, P. M., & Quiroz, B. (1995, March). Developing interpersonal relationships in the cultural contexts of individualism and collectivism. In C. Raeff (Chair). *Individualism and collectivism as cultural contexts for developing different modes of independence and interdependence.* Symposium presented at the Biennial Meeting of SRCD, March 29, 1995, Indianapolis, IA.

Ramirez, III, M., & Castaneda, A. (1974). *Cultural democracy, bicognitive development, and education.* New York: Academic Press.

Rothstein-Fisch, C., Greenfield, P. M., & Trumbull, E. (1999). Bridging Cultures for immigrant Latino students. *Educational Leadership*, 56(7), 64–67.

Rothstein-Fisch, C., Trumbull, E., Quiroz, B., & Greenfield. P. M. (1997, June). *Bridging Cultures in the classroom.* Poster presentation at the Jean Piaget Society. Santa Monica, CA.

Rothstein-Fisch, C., Trumbull, E., Quiroz, B., & Greenfield, P. M. (1998), *Supporting teachers to bridge cultures for immigrant Latino students: A model for professional development.* Research Report. San Francisco: WestEd.

Rutherford, B. (Ed.) (1995). *Creating family/school partnerships.* Columbus, OH: National Middle School Association.

Sagor, R. (1991). What Project LEARN reveals about collaborative action research. *Educational Leadership*, 48(6), 6–10.

Schaefer, R. J. (1967). *The school as a center of inquiry*. New York: Harper and Row.

Schön, D. (1983). *The reflective practitioner*. New York: Basic Books.

Seeley, D. S. (1993). A new paradigm for parent involvement. In N. F. Chavkin (Ed.), *Families and schools in a pluralistic society* (pp. 229–234). New York, NY: State University of New York Press.

Shakespear, E. (1999). What I'd tell a White gal: What my Black male students taught me about race and schooling. In S. W. Freedman, E. R. Simons, J. S. Kalnin, A. Casareno, & The M-CLASS Teams. *Inside city schools: Investigating literacy in multicultural classrooms* (pp. 77–88), New York: Teachers College Press; and Urbana, IL: National Council of Teachers of English.

Shulman, L. (1987). Knowledge and teaching: Foundations of the new reform. *Harvard Educational Review*, 51, 1–22.

Simich-Dudgeon, C. (1993). Increasing student achievement through teacher knowledge about parent involvement. In N. F. Chavkin (Ed.), *Families and schools in a pluralistic society* (pp. 189–203). New York, NY: State University of New York Press.

Simons, E. R., with Daniels, K., Yearwood, J., & Walker, D. (1999). Diversifying curriculum in multicultural classrooms: "You can't be what you can't see." In S. W. Freedman, E. R. Simons, J. S. Kalnin, A. Casareno, & The M-CLASS Teams. *Inside city schools: Investigating literacy in multicultural classrooms* (pp.142–160). New York: Teachers College Press; and Urbana, IL: National Council of Teachers of English.

Soul food (1997). 20th Century Fox.

Sparks-Langer, G. M., & Colton, A. B. (1991). Synthesis of research on teachers' reflective thinking. *Educational Leadership*, 48(6), 37–44.

Stand and deliver (1988). Warner Bros.

Stein, M. K., Smith, M. S., & Silver, E. A. (1999). The development of professional developers: Learning to assist teachers in new settings in new ways. *Harvard Educational Review*, 69(3), 237–269.

Stewart, E. C. (1971). *American cultural patterns: A cross-cultural perspective*. Pittsburgh, PA: Regional Council for International Education.

Stigler, J. W., & Perry, M. (1988). Mathematics learning in Japanese, Chinese, and American classrooms. In G. B. Saxe & M. Gearhart (Eds.), *Children's mathematics. New directions for child development* No. 41 (pp. 27–54). San Francisco, CA: Jossey-Bass.

Storr, A. (1988). *Solitude: A return to the self*. New York: Free Press.

Suina, J. H., & Smolkin, L. B. (1994). From natal culture to school culture to dominant society culture: Supporting transitions for Pueblo Indian students. In P. M. Greenfield & R. Cocking (Eds.), *Cross-cultural roots of minority child development* (pp. 115–130). Hillsdale, NJ: Lawrence Erlbaum Associates.

child development (pp. 115–130). Hillsdale, NJ: Lawrence Erlbaum Associates.

Tama, M.C., & Peterson, K. (1991). Achieving reflectivity through literature. *Educational Leadership*, 48(6), 22–24.

Tator, C., & Henry, F. (1991), *Multicultural education: Translating policy into practice*. Ottowa: Ministry of Multiculturalism.

Triandis, H. C. (1989). Cross-cultural studies of individualism and collectivism. *Nebraska symposium on motivation*, 37, 43–133.

Triandis, H., Brislin, R., & Hui, C. H. (1988). Cross-cultural training across the individualism-collective divide. *International Journal of Intercultural Relations*, 12, 269–289.

Trumbull, E., Greenfield, P. M., Rothstein-Fisch, C., & Maynard, A. (1999, April). *From altered perceptions to altered practice: Teachers bridge cultures in the classroom*. Paper presented at the Annual Meeting of the American Educational Research Association, Montreal, Quebec, Canada.

Trumbull, E., Rothstein-Fisch, C., & Greenfield, P. M. (1999). Bridging Cultures*: New approaches that work*. Knowledge brief. San Francisco: WestEd.

U.S. Department of Commerce, Bureau of the Census (1998), *Population estimates for States by race and Hispanic origin*. Population Estimates Program, Population Division, Washington, DC: U.S. Census Bureau.

U.S. Department of Commerce, Bureau of the Census (1999), *Current Population Reports, Series P-20, Level of enrollment below college for persons 3 to 24 years old, by control of school, metropolitan status, sex, race, and Hispanic origin*. Washington, DC: U.S. Census Bureau.

U.S. Department of Education (1994), *Strong families, strong schools*. Washington, DC: U.S. Government Printing Office.

Valdés, G. (1996). *Con respeto*. New York: Teachers College Press.

Weisner, T.S., & Gallimore, R. (1977). My brother's keeper: Child and sibling caretaking. *Current Anthropology*, 18(2), 169–190.

Winkelman, P. G. (1999). Family involvement in education: The apprehensions of student teachers. In M.S. Ammon (Ed.), *Joining Hands. Preparing teachers to make meaningful home-school connections* (pp. 790100). Sacramento, CA: California Department of Education Press.

Young, M. D. (1999). Multifocal educational policy research: Toward a method for enhancing traditional educational policy studies. *American Educational Research Journal*, 36 (4), 677–714.

Zaharlick, A. (1992). Ethnography in anthropology and its value for education. *Theory Into Practice*, 31(2), 116–125.

Zeichner, K. M., & D. P. Liston (1996), *Reflective teaching: An introduction*. Mahwah, NJ: Lawrence Erlbaum Associates.

Author Index

T

Tama, M. C., 103
Tator, C., 23
Taylor, S. I., 31
Todnem, G. R., 94
Touchstone Pictures, 103
Triandis, H. C., xv, 5, 11
Trumbull, E., 28, 49, 53, 75, 98, 121, 139, 141, 142, 143
20th Century Fox, 103

U

U.S. Department of Commerce xiv, xv
U.S. Department of Education, 28, 30

V

Valdés, G, 28, 34, 36, 38, 39, 41, 49, 89, 125
Van Tassell, M. A., 97, 124

W

Walker, D., 112
Warner Bros., 103
Wasson, R., 31
Weisner, T. S., 112
Whittaker, A., 98
Williams, D. L., 32, 46, 48
Winkelman, P. G, 46
Wolf, S., 98
Wong, I., 98
Wood, W., 112

Y

Yanez, E., 17
Yearwood, J., 112
Young, M. D., 32, 35

Z

Zaharlick, A., 104, 105, 108
Zeichner, K. M., 94, 95, 102, 124

Subject Index

C

D

Diversity
in American society, xiii-xiv
in the classroom, xiii-xv
in the teaching workforce, xiv-xv

E

Ethnicity
contrasted with culture, xv, 56
of student and teacher populations, xiii-xv

Ethnography
conducted by *Bridging Cultures* teachers, 85-87, 104, 106-108
defined, 103
educational vs. anthropological, 105
ethical concerns, 111-112
of Mexican immigrants, 110-111
in the M-CLASS Project, 112-113
guidelines for, 108-111
obtaining key information, 51, 52, 106, 108-109
teachers' engagement in, 52, 104-108

F

Families, *see also* Parents *and* Parent Involvement
informal interactions with, 76-78
involved in schooling, 29-33, 38-45, 80, 81-87
teachers' personal relationships with, 76-77, 81-83
values of, and education, 6-21, 35, 43-44

H

Home-school conflicts, 6-21
cognitive skills vs. social skills, 17-18
individual vs. group, 14-15
independence vs. helpfulness, 15-16
oral expression vs. respect for authority, 18-19
parents' roles vs. teachers' roles, 19-20
personal property vs. sharing, 20-21
praise vs. criticism, 16-17

Homework, 39-40, 50-51

I

M

P